Charles Dowding
Grow Together

Charles Dowding
Grow Together

50 planting partnerships to boost your harvests

Contents

HAPPY TOGETHER 6

BEST SOIL, BEST METHODS 11

Ways to grow together 12

Why no dig suits growing together 16

Key techniques 20

SEASONAL COMBINATIONS 29

Close spacings year round 30

SPRING 32

SUMMER 72

AUTUMN 124

Index 154

Resources 158

About the author 160

HAPPY TOGETHER

My first year of market gardening was 1983, the first time I had space to try new methods as well as supply customers. I was looking to maximize space efficiency and find plants that might grow well together to help achieve that aim.

A first experiment in interplanting

In May of that year I tried something different, in two beds of 5 x 1.5m (16½ x 5ft). I had transplanted Brussels sprouts at 60cm (24in) apart, and then was struck by the wide empty spaces between them while they were so small. One bed I left with 16 Brussels plants on their own, but in the neighbouring bed I planted 36 lettuces between the Brussels sprout plants.

I had never tried this and did not know what to expect; I worried the lettuce would compete with and slow the growth of the sprout plants. Then by June, something was very apparent. The Brussels with lettuce between were 50 per cent larger, and the lettuce were growing very nicely themselves, to harvest in early July. This was the first time I saw strong evidence of benefits to be had from interplanting.

Today, 43 years later, Homeacres is my fourth market garden. I've had opportunities to grow different combinations of plants with different timings using a range of spacings. Some have not been fruitful, while others have worked well. Those trials have led to the plant combinations in this book, all of which will help you maximize production, especially in small spaces, while reducing growing times.

In my 25 square metre (30 square yard) small garden, where I use and trial many "growing" together combinations.

How it works

In the gardening world I grew up with, the language was about competition between plants for space, water, and light. There was little acknowledgement of how plants can cooperate and benefit from association. Sometimes I trial combinations that feel almost outrageous, with new and very small plantings having little light or, it would appear, nutrition.

Small seedlings, I now see clearly, can start between much larger plants which are nearing the end of their life, on average within 4–5 weeks. The scarcely visible seedlings develop roots as much as new leaves, so when the larger plants are harvested and cleared, they grow rapidly. In the wild, seeds germinate and start life with a thicket of plants around them. It's a similar process, if more random than in our organized gardens. After a period of time, the new seedlings gain prominence, while older plants fade.

Beauty

Any beautiful and fully planted garden is an uplifting sight, and I feel plants prefer it compared to a monoculture, and to wider but empty spaces between. Beauty attracts us to a garden and that leads to a bonus for us, as well as the plants, especially when growing flowers among vegetables. You will breathe in microbes such as *Mycobacterium vaccae*, which lives in the soil. Our bodies use it to produce serotonin, which lifts the spirits.

I lay out my plot with minimum width for the paths, 40cm (16in) on average. That means vegetable leaves often overgrow the paths and all available sunlight is being used. The effect is incredibly lush and attractive. Summer visitors to Homeacres, when flowers are gorgeously prominent, often exclaim about its beauty and ask what the blooms are for. I tell them it's partly for our health and happiness, because a beautiful garden draws people into it.

Sunflowers are greedy plants, yet make good companions for many vegetables, and are a stunning addition to the summer garden.

Part 1

Best Soil, Best Methods

WAYS TO GROW TOGETHER

In nature, seedlings rarely start life in bare ground with open spaces between them. Small seedlings benefit from the proximity of neighbouring plants. Similarly, growing crops together takes advantage of how plants cooperate, rather than focusing on how they compete.

Transplants raised under cover (or seeds) can be planted between existing, larger plants that will soon finish, allowing space for the new plants to grow. This gives you a head start, adding valuable time to the growing season. The young plants under cover may be several weeks old, adding equivalent time to the season. You are overlapping crops for this extra time, rather than waiting for one to finish before starting the next.

For those of us with relatively short growing seasons, this creates new possibilities. Direct-sown lettuce can take 16 weeks to harvest, but transplanted three-week-old plants will be ready in 13 weeks. Then, after harvest, you'll still have time for a crop of beetroot. In addition, we are boosting life in the soil through enabling more photosynthesis, which brings extra carbon to feed microbes associating with plant roots.

COVER CROPPING

Cover crops are plants whose leaves cover the ground, so extra photosynthesis is bringing carbon into the soil. Cover crops mostly do not give a harvest, although vegetables and flowers can serve as cover crops if they provide dense leaf cover. The more leaf area over the soil, the more fertility is increased. It's another reason why growing together is such a powerful tool.

Companion plantings

Companion plantings grow close together, and help each other in ways not always understood. There is an interesting pointer about what makes a good association: vegetables and herbs that taste good when eaten together, tend to grow well together. Examples include basil and tomatoes, beetroot and onions, lettuce and salad rocket, dill and cucumbers. In fact, many of the combinations in this book!

Catch crop combinations

A catch crop matures rapidly, and is harvested before its neighbour or companion planting needs the space. The main planting needs to be at wide spacing, with its initial growth not too rapid. Few vegetables grow sufficiently fast for use as catch crops. Two main ones in spring are radish and turnips.

Succession using interplanting

Using transplants aids maximum use of small spaces, as you start plants off elsewhere and add time to your growing season. For example, you can multi-sow beetroot in late May to plant between onions at summer solstice. A month later the onions are being pulled, by when the clumps of beetroot are seven or eight weeks old and almost half grown. The result is a large beetroot harvest by the middle or end of autumn in ground that has already given a harvest of onions. A few interplants last longer, even for the whole life of both vegetables (see Leek between Celeriac, p.42).

Succession using intersowing

Traditionally, any direct sowing is made into clear ground, after a first planting has finished. With intersowing, you sow *between* plants still growing, which you know will finish within, say, a month. Often in early summer when we intersow, the soil is dry. Watering is for both new seeds and existing plants, resulting in a double use of the water.

Key benefits of growing together

Whichever type of planting combination used, there is the benefit of closer spacing. That results in better use of space, either through multi-sowing or intersowing and interplanting.

All plants that have sufficient light and moisture can be companions. You don't need a long table of likes and dislikes; it's more about non-interference and mutual support. See also Multi-sowing, below.

Support networks develop between plants. These are becoming more understood, in terms of roots linking to the foraging abilities of mycelial and bacterial networks in soil. These networks are fragile and are damaged by cultivation, even forking soil, hence the success of growing together in no dig soil (see p.16). Some of the results I describe in this book might not be applicable in soil that is dug regularly.

MULTI-SOWING

This is when small seeds are sown together in the same hole. I notice that traditional gardeners, on seeing clumps for the first time, cannot believe how such "space competition" might be successful. I see it as seedlings growing with their mates, and benefiting from proximity to other small seedlings, at the most vulnerable stage of their life. When transplanted as a clump, seedlings grow more strongly than if grown singly. I observe how the total harvest of vegetables such as beetroot, onions, radish, turnips, and certain leaf veg, is outstandingly high relative to the space used and time taken.

At the summer solstice we transplanted 18-day-old beetroot seedlings between lettuce, which continued cropping for another 24 days.

WHY NO DIG SUITS GROWING TOGETHER

In broad terms, no dig is how nature works. It involves minimal disturbance, while feeding the soil with organic matter (mulch or compost) on the surface. Digging tries to loosen the soil by breaking its structure and incorporating organic matter into the "rooting zone", but it also breaks existing biological networks.

A trial

At Homeacres, since 2012, I have run a two-bed trial, comparing a bed I dig alongside one I don't. Both receive the same amount of compost, incorporated into the dig soil and laid on the surface of the no dig. We set the same plants at the same time into both beds in every month between March and September, and eventual harvests are taken at the same time. Thirteen years of results show consistently that growth and harvest weight are higher with no dig, by around 11 per cent.

Organic matter

The organic matter in the soil consists of carbon-based molecules. These aggregate soil in various ways, and make it darker compared to deeper subsoil, which has less organic matter. Carbon compounds are the basis of fertility, and at Homeacres the soil from each bed of this trial has been analysed for carbon content. The bed I dig every year had 14 per cent carbon in January 2024, compared to 18 per cent carbon in soil of the no dig bed. Both beds received the same amount of compost during the trial's 12 years, until that point. The difference is a powerful pointer to explaining the success of a no dig approach, because it conserves the soil's vital building blocks for structure and fertility. With healthy soil, crop rotation is not necessary, and recently I learned that, in a biologically active soil, plant roots can adjust the pH in their vicinity, called the rhizosphere, to enable healthy growth.

Soil structure

Healthy soils have a stable structure and resist a certain amount of weight without collapsing. Organic matter in the soil holds air, moisture, and space for roots and organisms to travel. That's why with no dig you can put your feet on soil without squashing the air out. In contrast, digging will damage structure, meaning soil is not stable afterwards, although some maintain that the process improves soil conditions through introducing air.

How no dig works so well

No dig increases soil's biological activities in two key areas. The first is the mycelial network, invisible threads of fungi that help plant roots source food and moisture, in return for sugars provided by root hairs, the results of photosynthesis. Another is rhizophagy, the transference of nutrients into plant roots from bacteria, which are attracted to root hairs by the offer of sugars.

In summary, these processes provide nutrients accessible to plant roots as complex organic compounds, a food source more balanced than synthetic fertilizer. Plants grow faster and require more food when soil temperature rises, and there is sufficient moisture. This correlates with the actions of fungi and bacteria, which become more active in warm, moist conditions. A perfect match for healthy plant growth. For much more on this, see my book *No Dig*.

Overleaf: Early September garden. The beetroot in the foreground were transplanted on 29 April between garlic, six weeks before their harvest.

KEY TECHNIQUES

Sourcing seed

Buy reliable seed from a supplier you trust. You can also save seed of many vegetables, as long as they are not F1 selections. Home-saved seed germinates strongly as seeds are fresh and adapted somewhat to your garden.

Why raise as transplants?

Direct sowing is quick to do, but uses more space. In the first 3–4 weeks after sowing little happens and there are often pest problems as seedlings are vulnerable as they emerge. Under cover you have fewer pests and seedlings are unaffected by rough weather, with hundreds growing in just a small space. Many times I observe plants grow more strongly when transplanted rather than sown direct. There is something about the shock to a plant from being moved that stimulates stronger growth in the end. Note that carrots and parsnips *should* be direct sown, as they form tap roots that branch if damaged.

Phases of plant raising

Think of plant raising as two distinct phases: germination and growing on. Germination takes 5–12 days; growing on lasts around three weeks. Higher temperatures are required for germination than for growing on. Using house warmth for germination is efficient, with plants transferred to a greenhouse after you see green leaves.

During spring you need a greenhouse or polytunnel. I find cold frames less well suited because they don't stay warm and harbour slugs. Windowsills are useful in the first week of growing on; after that you need to use LED grow lights. I avoid traditional hardening off by taking plants straight from my greenhouse and popping them into the cold soil outside, covering with fleece if needed (see p.24).

What to sow when

Cold tolerant vegetables These include beetroot, broad beans, cabbage, calabrese, lettuce, onions, peas, and turnips. A frosty night in early spring won't kill these if they are in an unheated greenhouse or planted outside, so you can sow from mid-February.

Frost intolerant vegetables These include runner and French beans, courgettes, cucumbers, melons, sweetcorn, squashes, and tomatoes. It can be a disaster if you raise these too early and they are hit by frost. I sow tomatoes between 10 and 15 March and cucumbers in mid-April, later than some growers, but I follow the saying "In spring, sowings catch up". Runner and French beans are good to sow from 10 May under cover, or in late May, directly outside.

Potting mixes

Buy a general-purpose or multi-purpose potting mix, and use it for sowing seed as well as raising plants. It is hard to find good commercial mixes; the term "peat-free" is no indicator of quality, and you may find multi-purpose mixes full of wood, which must be sieved out before use. Purpose-made seed mixes are too low in nutrients for ongoing growth.

Mix your own blend

Homemade garden compost containing worms makes an excellent base for potting mix. When dry enough it can be sifted to 4mm ($\frac{1}{8}$in) for beautiful, soft compost, perfect for sowing seed. Adding this to a commercial potting mix at 10–50 per cent volume, I find, transforms it. Worm compost can be dense and sticky, with insufficient air for seedling roots, so adding lighter commercial potting mix and some vermiculite or perlite gives an open blend. Or use coir, which also provides great structure.

How to sow seeds

Cells with a 3cm (1¼in) diameter work well and are space-efficient. Drop individual seeds into the cells (unless you are multi-sowing, see p.14). Cover with compost as deep as the seeds are wide; tiny seeds such as lettuce can be surface sown or covered with a dusting of vermiculite. Water with a fine rose from above, every day if sunny, or every second day at germination stage. In the summer heat of a greenhouse, put newly sown trays under a bench for 3–4 days to keep direct sun off emerging seedlings.

Seeds with uncertain germination levels such as some brassicas, chicory, and lettuce, and tiny seeds that are hard to handle, I scatter on top of potting mix in a shallow seed tray. At the two-leaf stage I lift a clump of seedlings using a pencil, and peel off plants, one by one, handling by the leaves. I pop each seedling into a pencil-shaped, deep hole in each cell, burying any long stem to reduce legginess.

When to transplant

It is easy to leave transplants too long in their modules. Watch carefully and plant them out before you see leaves starting to yellow at the bottom of each plant, and this includes cotyledons (seed leaves). Yellowing is a sign your seedlings can't grow any more. Transplants can also run out of growing space, reaching up to the light with fragile stems. Hence, my advice not to sow too early. Sow at the right time and plants will come ready at an appropriate moment to plant, even while quite small.

Beetroot in late spring, 10 days after they were multi-sown.

HOW LONG DO I KEEP TRANSPLANTS?

This depends mostly on the vegetable. Radishes can be transplanted in less than three weeks. They grow fast, and then do better in the ground rather than having roots restricted. At the other extreme, celeriac can take six weeks, as seed is tiny and slow. Lettuces, onions, and most brassicas are more typical, taking on average four weeks in spring until you plant out.

Sometimes, and especially for warmth-loving vegetables, it's worth potting on, into a 7cm (2¾in) pot, with the same mix you used to fill module trays. Make a hole in the potting mix deeper than the root ball is long, because usually there's a stem, which is best below surface level, in order to keep plants sturdy and strong.

How to plant out

I always dib holes deep enough so that stems are below ground level, with the first true leaves at surface level. Drop the root ball into your hole and, with a finger placed either side of the stem, gently push the plant down to ensure its root ball has good contact with the surrounding soil and compost. Don't fill the hole, as the action of watering (and rain) moves surface compost into holes over time, and beforehand they serve as water hollows for each root ball.

Using fleece

Anything I transplant between late March and early May I cover with fleece, which allows light and air to enter, while holding sunshine warmth close to the plants. It offers protection from strong winds, and is a barrier against pests. It is more fragile than mesh and develops holes over its lifespan of a few years. Mesh is stronger and more expensive, serving to keep out larger animals and birds year-round, and is useful against insects in summer. Plant-based products are available (see p.158).

Last frost dates

Before transplanting frost-intolerant plants outside, you'll need to know your location's average last frost date. Watch weather forecasts closely. Over much of the UK, last frosts are roughly the middle of May, but local knowledge is needed, as it can be later. Fleece will help avoid overnight damage if temperatures do not fall too low.

Dropping a bean plant into a dibbed hole, between lettuce due to finish leaf harvests in four weeks.

Pests and diseases

The starting point for pest and disease control is to know which are most likely to cause you problems. Decide which crops you need to protect before damage happens. Sowing seed at the right time is a top method for avoiding certain pests. Flea beetles are often a problem on summer-sown brassicas. Salad rocket is especially vulnerable and I find it's best sown in late summer for autumn harvests, by when the flea beetle season has passed. Other brassicas may be better sown extra early such as cabbage in February to give cabbage hearts in June, before flea beetles and caterpillars are common. Flea beetles are less keen on old and tougher leaves, so protect young brassicas with mesh before they grow too tall to cover, to prevent most damage.

Managing problems No dig techniques (see p.16) maintain healthy soil, which provides strong, healthy plants. Pests and diseases generally affect weaker plants, so remember to mulch all soil every year. Reduce disease by removing the worst-affected material to compost. Photosynthesis mostly happens in the newest leaves, so you can remove diseased lower leaves, which also reduces slug numbers and creates space for a further crop. Sometimes it's about tolerating what may look like a problem, but is not. Courgettes always suffer from mildew on older, lower leaves by late summer, but the young leaves stay healthy and they are doing most of the photosynthesis.

Weeding

I recommend checking regularly to catch weeds while small and easy to pull cleanly. Direct-sown crops often go into the soil before weeds have had a chance to germinate. Therefore, using transplants a few weeks later allows you to pull or hoe small weeds just before planting. Regular weeding also allows you to notice and react to other problems.

Multi-sown turnips to transplant between dwarf French beans in early September.

LEARN TO WING IT

Flexibility is key if you want to take full advantage of the potential your vegetable garden offers. This is partly why I don't practise crop rotation. I keep raising young vegetable plants through the season, and from May onwards I'll often walk around the garden with a tray of transplants looking for gaps with the potential for crops that could follow or overlap with existing ones. This is how I develop many interplant combinations. Look for plants that will finish within 4–6 weeks and see if there is room to slot seedlings in between them, allowing them to be established by the time the earlier crop is removed.

Part 2

Seasonal combinations

CLOSE SPACINGS YEAR ROUND

A planting concept rather than a prescription, this principle is the first of my 50 planting partnerships. I advocate growing vegetables closer together than commonly advised, by combining many techniques that I practise and recommend, such as the five special techniques below.

I have been cropping a garden area of 25 square metres (30 square yards) since 2013 to see how multi-cropping a relatively small space can work. This is vegetable gardening on a scale many people can relate to, with issues often experienced in back gardens. The area has shade on three sides and a neighbour's trees are rooting into the garden soil, reducing growth in dry weather. Nonetheless, thanks to close spacing, replanting straight after every harvest, and interplanting where possible, the annual harvest is 80–110kg (176–243lb) of vegetables and soft fruit. I minimize the space between plants, as they benefit from being in close proximity.

No dig

An undisturbed soil structure enables healthy root growth and stronger plants. Weed pressure is reduced, so that crops such as onions are easy to maintain weed free, even at close spacing (see p.16).

Multi-sowing

Sowing several seeds together within the same module gives clumps of plants rather than individuals. Seedlings go in the ground with their mates, and fill the space more quickly. I do this with many root vegetables including onions, beetroot, turnips, and radishes (see p.14).

Succession planting

As one crop finishes, another can follow seamlessly, sown or planted into the same space. Some of my favourite examples are purple sprouting

Spinach, transplanted three weeks earlier, under cordon (indeterminate) tomatoes, which are still cropping heavily.

broccoli followed by courgettes, broad beans followed by beetroot, peas followed by carrots, and spring cabbage (from an autumn planting) followed by tomatoes.

Overlapping plantings

Get a new crop into the ground before the previous one has finished. For example, the spaces between lettuces can be exploited by popping seeds of French beans in between (see p.100), while ridge cucumbers can be slotted close to peas and strawberries (see p.90).

Interplanting

Plant two crops together in the same space, in many cases taking advantage of complementary growing habits. Examples include sowing radishes and carrots together (see p.76), and leeks with celeriac (see p.42).

CLOSE SPACINGS YEAR ROUND

BRUSSELS SPROUT
between CARROT

COMPANION TYPE: OVERLAP (4–8 weeks)

These two crops appear an unlikely combination but in my experience they always grow really well together. The Brussels sprouts should be ready for transplanting in June, just after the carrots sown in early spring have started to crop. Then a long period of harvesting carrots provides increasing space for developing Brussels sprout plants.

Brussels grow strongly in the company of carrots, I suspect due to mycelial relationships between the roots. As with most other beds, this one receives 3cm (1¼in) new compost in late autumn, and I grow nothing there through winter, for best germination of carrots in early spring, with few slugs. The soil is not bare in winter as it's covered with compost. Sow carrots around the time of spring equinox, and choose an early, quick-growing cultivar, as you don't want them to linger before the Brussels grow large.

Growing and planting Brussels sprouts

Sow Brussels under cover in early May. I find 10 May is the cut-off date where I garden, so that the plants have time to develop fully. Brussels need a long season, and you want reasonably sized plants; I get good results from transplants in 7cm (2¾in) pots, after sowing in small module cells. In summer, water sprouts twice a week but not the carrots, which will be sweeter if kept on the dry side. Carrots are ready for a first harvest in mid-June. Pull the carrots at 60cm (24in) intervals, enough to make a football-sized space for the new Brussels plants. Every few days, pull a few more around the planting hole's circumference to make more space for

By early July the interplanted Brussels sprouts are rising above the carrots.

Brussels. Continue until the end of July; any later and carrots get tougher and may start to split. By this stage, your Brussels will be 60cm (24in) tall. In October tie Brussels to 1.2m (4ft) stakes to support them through wet, windy conditions.

GROWING TIP

I keep a mesh cover over carrots to protect against root fly, and it also keeps insects off Brussels plants until the end of July, by which time they are too tall for a cover. Wider mesh may then be installed, ideally sturdy enough to deter pigeons.

CULTIVARS

BRUSSELS SPROUT

F1 hybrids are more reliable for growing tight sprouts, with less "blowing".

'Brigitte' F1 Tall variety ideal for cropping November to January, 1.2m (4ft) high.

'Crispus' F1 Early cultivar cropping from September to November, 75cm (30in) high.

'Trafalgar' F1 Heavy-cropping sprout for a January to March harvest, 1.2m (4ft) high.

CARROT

These are all fast growing.

'Amsterdam Forcing 3' Long, thin carrots and super-early to crop.

'Nantes Milan 2' Sweet, quick-growing, early carrot with rounded cylindrical roots.

'Norwich' F1 Second early Nantes-type carrot with good flavour and vigour.

KEY INFORMATION

BRUSSELS SPROUT

Seed to harvest: 20–30 weeks **Seed to transplanting:** 6 weeks **Position:** Sunny and sheltered **Spacing** 60cm (24in) **Hardiness:** Fully hardy

CARROT

Seed to harvest: 11 weeks
Position: Sun or part shade **Spacing:** 1 carrot per 1cm (½in), rows 22cm (8½in) apart
Hardiness: Fully hardy

TIMINGS

BRUSSELS SPROUT

Sowing: Early May **Transplanting:** Mid-June
Harvesting: Late September to March (depending on variety)

CARROT

Sowing: Late March to early April
Harvesting: 10–17 weeks after sowing

ALTERNATIVE CHOICES

Kale, autumn cabbage, beetroot, and salad onions can be transplanted between carrots.

Carrots continue to swell nicely during the overlap.

CORIANDER *between* GARLIC

COMPANION TYPE: OVERLAP (4–8 weeks)

Garlic is ideal for planting between, and also for adding between winter-cropping vegetables under cover. In this example, well suited to smaller spaces, you are sowing or planting coriander as an overlapping crop between rows of garlic planted as cloves in autumn.

Coriander is among many vegetables or flowers you can start growing between rows of garlic, which will then finish within 4–8 weeks (you can also try lettuce, beetroot, carrots, parsley, dill, and celeriac). The upright growth habit of garlic allows plenty of light to reach newly added coriander plants. The garlic roots are busy in the soil, but mycelial association is good between the two crops because we can see how well new plants establish very close to the stems of garlic. Another option is to interplant garlic in October between winter salads under cover, which will grow and crop for a long period while garlic is slowly starting until February, and then growing strongly (see p.133).

GROWING TIP

Plant your garlic in rows so that you can also set the new coriander plants in rows between, for quicker picking, and weeding.

CULTIVARS

CORIANDER

'Calypso' Compact, low-growing cultivar that is slow to bolt.

'Cruiser' My number one cultivar, does not flower quickly and bears broad, dark green leaves.

'Leisure' Lush, large-leaved selection, slow to bolt, with good flavour.

GARLIC

'Early Purple Wight' Softneck garlic forming large, well-flavoured bulbs as early as the end of May.

'Messidrome' Easy to peel softneck with fat bulbs and top flavour, ready from mid-June.

'Morado' A hardneck with strong flavour. Suited to cooler climates and comes ready from late June.

Coriander between garlic in early May.

KEY INFORMATION

CORIANDER

Seed to harvest: 6–8 weeks **Seed to transplanting:** 3 weeks, or sow in lines between the garlic **Position:** Sun or semi-shade **Spacing:** 7cm (2¾in) apart in rows **Hardiness:** Moderately frost hardy

GARLIC

Planting to harvest: 32–36 weeks **Position:** Sun **Spacing:** 30cm (12in) between rows, 10cm (4in) between each clove **Hardiness:** Hardy

TIMINGS

CORIANDER

Sowing: Mid-August direct, and to early September under cover **Transplanting:** September **Harvesting:** October to March (if plants survive winter)

GARLIC

Planting: (From cloves) Mid-October **Harvesting:** 30 May–20 June; timings vary with garlic type, climate, and incidence of rust disease (see p.83)

TOMATO *between* GARLIC

COMPANION TYPE: OVERLAP (3–4 weeks)

This easy combination can be used both outdoors and under cover and is an efficient pairing for small spaces. The timings of the two crops work perfectly, garlic growing large in its final weeks as young tomato plants establish. I find garlic is best managed in rows, allowing greater opportunities for overlap-planting combinations.

The timing of tomato planting outside, which I do from mid-May, proves ideal for slotting the plants between and close to garlic, which will be harvested about a month later, when the tomato plants are already filling the space. In the greenhouse and polytunnel, by the time for planting tomatoes in early May, the October-planted garlic plants are so big that visitors often mistake them for leeks. Under cover I grow just one row of garlic along the middle of beds which are cropping winter salads (see p.133).

ALTERNATIVE CHOICES

Outdoors, you could try growing tomatoes between spring onions rather than garlic. In early May, harvest enough spring onions to make space for tomato plants among them. This combination is a particularly nice example of how vegetables that taste good together, also grow well together.

CULTIVARS

TOMATO

'Crimson Crush' F1 Blight-resistant with large fruit, going towards beefsteak, and crimson coloured. Decent flavour and often a high yield when grown outdoors.

'Orange Wellington' F1 Strong grower with medium to large beefsteak fruit, yellow-orange, and with excellent flavour.

'Sakura' F1 Good yields of larger cherry tomatoes, dark red with a sweet flavour.

'Sungold' F1 Extraordinarily fruity, sweet flavour. Ripens early under cover.

GARLIC

Softneck garlic works best here, because it harvests earlier than hardneck.

'Germidour' Large bulbs for a June harvest.

'Provence Wight' Large bulbs often ready by late May.

'Rhapsody Wight' Large, stores well, and harvests in mid- to late June.

KEY INFORMATION

TOMATO

Seed to harvest: 15–19 weeks **Seed to transplanting:** 6–8 weeks **Position:** Full sun **Spacing:** 45–50cm (18–20in) **Hardiness:** Frost tender

GARLIC

Planting to harvest: 32–36 weeks **Position:** Sun **Spacing:** 30cm (12in) between rows, 10cm (4in) between each plant **Hardiness:** Hardy

TIMINGS

TOMATO

Sowing: Mid-March (under cover)
Transplanting: Early May (under cover) to late May (outdoors) **Harvesting:** July to early October

GARLIC

Sowing: October **Harvesting:** 5 June under cover, 10–20 June outside

Tomatoes, marigolds, and checking garlic maturity in late May.

CELERIAC *between* GARLIC

COMPANION TYPE: OVERLAP (3–5 weeks)

If you already grow celeriac, this combination with garlic proves a useful and productive overlap. Garlic is easy to plant between, and its harvest happens just as the celeriac is beginning to grow strongly.

I planted my garlic the previous autumn, in rows across the bed. Garlic is almost mature by early June, a trait that proves helpful for the celeriac, which by that time is beginning to extend its roots. Early-cropping garlic cultivars can be ready to remove by the end of May. Plant celeriac around 10 May, four across a 1.5m (5ft) bed or three across a 1.2m (4ft) bed. This will allow it enough space to mature and make decent-sized bulbs by late October, before Septoria disease might damage plants. Many other vegetables can be sown between garlic, such as carrots, or transplanted, such as beetroot, lettuce, broccoli, dill, coriander, and parsley.

CULTIVARS

CELERIAC

'Asterix' F1 Early to mature cultivar with good yields and a rounded bulb.

'Monet' F1 Tasty, early-maturing celeriac with some resistance to bolting and Septoria.

'Prinz' Fine variety with light-skinned bulbs and good bolting resistance.

GARLIC See p.39.

KEY INFORMATION

CELERIAC

Seed to harvest: 30–38 weeks **Seed to transplanting:** 8–9 weeks **Position:** Full sun or part shade **Spacing:** 35–40cm (14–16in) **Hardiness:** Hardy to −10°C (14°F)

GARLIC See p.39.

Celeriac just transplanted between garlic on 12 May.

TIMINGS

CELERIAC

Sowing: 15–20 March (under cover)
Transplanting: 10–25 May **Harvesting:** Late October to early December

GARLIC

Planting: (From cloves) mid-October
Harvesting: 30 May–20 June; timings vary with garlic type, climate, and incidence of rust disease (see p.83)

GROWING TIP

I use a trowel to harvest the garlic, cutting close to its roots so as to ease it out without disturbing the celeriac. The celeriac then grows unchecked all summer for harvesting through autumn.

LEEK *between* CELERIAC

COMPANION TYPE: OVERLAP (20–28 weeks between planting and cropping the leeks)

This attractive pairing teams the blue-green strappy foliage of leeks with the glossy green leaves of celeriac, both transplanted in late spring. The aim is not to provide a succession of crops, but to combine two vegetables in a way that benefits both, increasing the total harvest.

Both are raised under glass. In mid-March, celeriac is surface sown in a small seed tray covered with a sheet of glass, seedlings pricked out into 3cm (1¼in) modules around a month after germinating, and grown on. I multi-sow leeks in early April, 4–5 seeds per module, which saves time and space. Transplanting before the middle of May is ideal for both. I allow more room than usual between rows of celeriac to accommodate leeks. I plant the celeriac in three rows along a 1.2m (4ft) bed, with each celeriac 40cm (16in) apart, to allow space for two rows of leeks between. Multi-sown leeks are transplanted with each clump 20–25cm (8–10in) apart.

You can harvest both vegetables at a similar time if an autumn-cropping leek is chosen, such as 'Autumn Mammoth 2', or harvest from July if you grow 'Jolant'. The beauty of leeks is how you can crop them at any stage,

---

ALTERNATIVE CHOICES

Spring onions are excellent and can be multi-sown in late February and March under cover; they will be ready to harvest in May and June, earlier than leeks. They take up less room and work well in small spaces.

By early October, both leeks and celeriac can be harvested.

including as young veg. Removing leeks gives space for celeriac to fill out and grow through October. Where leaf miner flies are prevalent, any later harvests of leeks will likely be damaged by their maggots. I don't cover celeriac in autumn, as that holds in moisture and increases the incidence of Septoria. Usually, it arrives in November, so I harvest my celeriac just before.

Crop cover bonus

During spring and very early summer, both crops benefit from a mesh cover to keep pests off; sap-sucking aphids can twist and deform celeriac foliage, and Allium leaf miner is spring flying and affects leeks. I take the cover off in June, when there are more predators to eat any aphids, and leaf miner is dormant in summer.

CULTIVARS

LEEK

'Autumn Mammoth 2 Hannibal' Short, stout variety for cropping from October.

'Bulgarian Giant' Very tall, slender, quick-growing leek, harvested from late summer.

'Jolant' Excellent variety with tall shanks and a long harvest season from late August into December.

CELERIAC See p.40.

KEY INFORMATION

LEEK

Seed to harvest: 24–32 weeks **Seed to transplanting:** 6 weeks **Position:** Sun **Spacing:** Multi-sown clumps 20–25cm (8–10in), individual plants 10cm (4in) **Hardiness:** Fully hardy

CELERIAC See p.40.

TIMINGS

LEEK

Sowing: Early April **Transplanting:** Early to mid-May **Harvesting:** 15–32 weeks for leeks (can harvest earlier as young leeks)

CELERIAC

Sowing: Mid-March **Transplanting:** Early to mid-May **Harvesting:** 28–32 weeks

Three months after setting out small plants of leeks and celeriac.

Interplanted leeks and celeriac in early July. We watered only the leeks, but the celeriac also benefited.

CELERIAC *between* LETTUCE

COMPANION TYPE: OVERLAP (5–6 weeks)

This straightforward combination gives great results. Leaf lettuce sown under cover is transplanted in well-spaced rows, allowing space for a later planting of young celeriac.

Celeriac transplants in the middle of May are small and grow slowly at first, so can be planted between any vegetable which will finish within 4–6 weeks. Lettuce harvested regularly for its outer leaves makes an easy choice, as does garlic (see p.39). Sow lettuce in late winter under cover and plant out in 30cm (12in) rows across the bed, giving room between each row to pop in the celeriac. I aim for three celeriac plants across a 1.2m (4ft) bed, for large bulbs, or four for smaller ones. Correct timing of sowing celeriac is vital: sow too early and they risk bolting in summer; sow too late, and the bulbs won't be large enough to harvest and store in autumn.

CULTIVARS

CELERIAC See p.40.
LETTUCE See p.75.

KEY INFORMATION

CELERIAC See p.40.

LETTUCE
Seed to harvest: 8–10 weeks **Seed to transplanting:** 4–5 weeks **Position:** Sun or part shade **Spacing:** Rows 30cm (12in) apart, plants 20cm (8in) apart **Hardiness:** Hardy

TIMINGS

CELERIAC
Sowing: 15–20 March (under cover)
Transplanting: 10–25 May **Harvesting:** Late October to early December

LETTUCE
Sowing: Late February (under cover)
Transplanting: Late March to early April
Harvesting: Late April to early July

Celeriac between lettuce in mid-June, with two to three more weeks of picking the lettuce before it flowers.

FENNEL *between* SPINACH

COMPANION TYPE: OVERLAP (4–6 weeks)

This planting overlaps true spinach sown the previous August with Florence fennel transplanted in mid-March. The spinach crops for 4–5 weeks more, after which the fennel grows strongly.

Between overwintered spinach I transplanted fennel seedlings from module trays into dibbed holes. I had sown the fennel in mid-February on a hotbed in my greenhouse. (See pp.86–89 for planting fennel in late summer, from a July sowing.) Young fennel plants are fragile so I grow extra in case they get eaten, and place fleece over transplants. In mild weather, crop small spinach leaves from mid-February. It helps to do so because letting leaves grow large reduces space for the fennel. The spinach crops until early May, when I cut them down or twist them out, leaving the roots in place. In June I transplant French beans between the fennel (see pp.94–95). You can also plant lettuce or multi-sown spring onions between spinach, instead of fennel.

CULTIVARS

FLORENCE FENNEL See p.88.
SPINACH See p.104.

KEY INFORMATION

FLORENCE FENNEL See p.88.
SPINACH See p.104.

TIMINGS

FLORENCE FENNEL

Sowing: Late February (under cover with some heat) **Transplanting:** Late March
Harvesting: June until solstice

SPINACH

Sowing: Mid-August (under cover; do not delay sowing, as plants too small going into winter will not give you much harvest)
Transplanting: Late August
Harvesting: October to early May

Fennel recently transplanted between overwintered spinach, early April.

GROWING TIP

Regular picking of the spinach is important; older leaves can attract slugs. Spread 1cm (½in) compost between spinach plants in mid-March, just before transplanting the fennel.

EARLY SPINACH *between* POTATO

COMPANION TYPE: OVERLAP (4–9 weeks, depending on when you plant your potatoes)

True spinach can be planted in early spring, with plants bolting from mid-May. This is ideal for overlapping with potatoes, which grow little for 2–3 weeks after planting in mid-spring, allowing spinach space to develop.

Spinach plants are cold-tolerant and can be sown under cover in late February for planting out in mid- to late March, before seed potatoes go in. I cover my young spinach with fleece to get them going. Plant the potatoes during April in two rows along a 1.2m (4ft) bed, in between the spinach. You could also grow radishes or turnips between the potatoes (see p.60).

CULTIVARS

SPINACH

'Amazon' F1 Fast growing with dark green leaves.

'Emilia' F1, **'Medania'**, and **'Missouri' F1** (see p.104).

POTATO See p.61.

KEY INFORMATION

SPINACH See p.104.

POTATO

Seed to harvest: 11 weeks, (second earlies), 16 weeks (maincrop) **Position:** Full sun **Spacing:** 45–50cm (18–20in) **Hardiness:** Not frost hardy

TIMINGS

SPINACH

Sowing: Mid-February to early March (under cover) **Transplanting:** Mid- to late March **Harvesting:** Late April to early June

POTATO

Planting seed potatoes: Early to mid-April (second earlies and maincrop potatoes) **Harvesting:** Early to mid-July (second earlies); August (maincrop)

By early June, potatoes are starting to fill the space while spinach gives final harvests.

GROWING TIP

Sow spinach early for a good harvest before it is overgrown by potato leaves. Opt for a second early or maincrop potato cultivar as first earlies might crowd out the spinach.

SPRING ONION *between* BEETROOT

COMPANION TYPE: OVERLAP (5–8 weeks), catch crop

While beetroot establish I like to slot spring onions in between. They overlap well thanks to their upright growth, with leaves that stand clear of the beetroot, and they are ready for cropping just before the beetroot need all the space.

The success of this easy combination relies on raising transplants of both veg in early spring. They take about four weeks until ready to plant. Multi-sow at the same time so that you can transplant both, any time from mid-April to mid-June. I pop 10 onion seeds in each module, which gives me perhaps eight plants, and 3 seeds of beetroot for growing four in each clump. Beetroot are the main harvest so plant them first, on the square. Next find space in between for the spring onions. By harvest time, no more than eight weeks after transplanting, there is almost total leaf cover, with a nice result of blanching the spring onion stems. The beetroot will start their long period of harvest a few weeks after you pull the last spring onions.

ALTERNATIVE CHOICES

Try swapping beetroot for celeriac; much of the detail is the same although the celeriac need wider spacing, at 35cm (14in). See also p.42 for an even longer interplant using alliums.

CULTIVARS

SPRING ONION

'Ishikura' Selection of *Allium fistulosum* ("bunching onion") with long, straight stems that don't make bulbs. Avoid harvesting this late or the leaves suffer rust and mildew.

'Tipika' Quick to grow and easy to peel.

'White Lisbon' Popular cultivar with long white stems maturing into bulbs.

BEETROOT

'Boltardy' Popular, bolt-resistant, flavoursome, and early cropping.

'Boston' Early crops of attractive, rounded, dark red roots.

'Jannis' Early cropping with deep purple, sweet, rounded roots.

KEY INFORMATION

SPRING ONION

Seed to harvest: 8–12 weeks **Seed to transplanting:** 3–4 weeks **Position:** Sun or part shade **Spacing:** 30cm (12in) **Hardiness:** Hardy to spring frosts

BEETROOT

Seed to harvest: 10–16 weeks **Seed to transplanting:** 3–4 weeks **Position:** Sun or part shade **Spacing:** 30cm (12in) between multi-sown clumps **Hardiness:** Hardy

TIMINGS

SPRING ONION

Sowing: Mid-March to early May (under cover) **Transplanting:** Early April to late May **Harvesting:** Mid-May to early August

BEETROOT

Sowing: Mid-March to early May (under cover) **Transplanting:** April to mid-June **Harvesting:** July to October

Overleaf: Early August harvest of salad onions, which were transplanted with beetroot in June (left). By late summer there are few spaces available and that's why interplanting is so worthwhile (right).

MELON *between* BEETROOT

COMPANION TYPE: OVERLAP (2–4 weeks)

This overlap planting for growing under cover in a greenhouse or polytunnel combines two contrasting crops. Melons for harvesting in late summer can be planted out to establish before much of the early sown beetroot crop has been picked.

One year I had a planting of 20 multi-sown clumps of beetroot in a new polytunnel, grown under cover for an early crop. As the beet harvest would not be complete until June, there was a month of overlap with melons that I transplanted in the middle of May, followed by careful harvest of the remaining beetroot. The melons can be planted 1m (3ft) apart, in space created by twisting out a clump of beetroot. This allows the young melons to get into the ground and establish without having to wait for the spring crop to finish. The melons can either ramble across the ground or be trained up strings.

CULTIVARS

MELON

'Emir' F1 Elongated Charentais-type with orange flesh, early ripening with great flavour.

'Lottie' F1 Slightly later, sweet, orange-fleshed cantaloupe with smaller fruits.

'Ogen' Cantaloupe with striped, greenish-yellow fruits and green flesh.

BEETROOT See p.53.

KEY INFORMATION

MELON

Seed to harvest: 18–24 weeks **Seed to transplanting:** 6 weeks **Position:** Bright, warm polytunnel or greenhouse **Spacing:** Plants 1m (3ft) apart **Hardiness:** Frost tender

BEETROOT See p.53.

TIMINGS

MELON

Sowing: Late March, for potting on mid-April (with heat, under cover)
Transplanting: Early to mid-May
Harvesting: August to September

BEETROOT

Sowing: Mid-February (under cover with heat; beetroot sown early without warmth will bolt) **Transplanting:** Mid-March
Harvesting: Early May to June

GROWING TIP

Melons need warmth to flourish and crop well, so don't be tempted to sow them too early. Note that watermelons need more heat and are suitable for warm climates only.

ASPARAGUS *interplanted with* TURNIP

COMPANION TYPE: OVERLAP (12 weeks, lifespan of the turnips)

Perennial asparagus takes up to four years to establish before you can harvest. In the first two years I like to interplant with early maturing crops such as turnips. By the third, asparagus needs more moisture and its roots will fill the ground.

I plant one row of asparagus up the middle of a bed 1–1.2m (3–4ft) wide, leaving space either side for subsequent growth. Asparagus can be raised from seed or planted from crowns. During their first year, I find they benefit from companion planting; spinach, lettuce, beetroot, and spring onions, which harvest in the first half of the year. Turnips make a perfect option in the second year, multi-sown under cover in late winter then planted out in early spring. You'll have a harvest by the middle of May, then keep the bed clear to give asparagus all the moisture and food in the soil. In September, even with established asparagus beds, you can plant or sow green manures and cover crops on either side of the central row, such as broad beans.

ALTERNATIVE CHOICES

Veg that mature before the middle of summer are well suited for interplanting between first year asparagus; possibilities are early carrots, Florence fennel, and radish.

CULTIVARS

ASPARAGUS

Open pollinated plants produce fruiting female stems that need removing in autumn.

'Connover's Colossal' Widely grown, open pollinated.

'Gijnlim' and **'Backlim'** All-male selections. Productive and well-flavoured.

'Stewart's Purple' Impressive, sweet, purple-flushed spears. Open pollinated.

TURNIP

Hakurei turnips are the most tasty option and mature rapidly too.

'Purple Top Milan' A traditional choice, but less sweet or juicy than 'Tokyo Cross'.

'Sweet Bell' F1 Quick-to-grow crops of baby turnips.

'Tokyo Cross' F1 Simply the best; fast-growing Hakurei with beautiful white skin, incredibly sweet and crunchy.

KEY INFORMATION

ASPARAGUS

Crown or seed to harvest: 3 years **Seed to transplanting:** 12 weeks **Position:** Sun **Spacing:** 60cm (2ft) **Hardiness:** Hardy, but early spears may be damaged by spring frost

TURNIP

Seed to harvest: 12 weeks
Seed to transplanting: 3–4 weeks
Position: Sun **Spacing:** Multi-sown clumps 30cm (12in) apart, 4–5 plants per clump
Hardiness: Hardy

TIMINGS

ASPARAGUS

Sowing: February to March **Transplanting:** June to July; alternatively plant crowns, March to April, which may bring harvesting forward by a year **Harvesting:** End April, May, and June until solstice

TURNIP

Sowing: Mid- to late February
Transplanting: End of March
Harvesting: May

TURNIP *and* RADISH *between* POTATO *and* PEA

COMPANION TYPE: CATCH CROP (4–6 weeks overlap)

This grouping makes full use of growing space before the bulkier potato plants need it, so is great for small plots. Radishes and turnips come to harvest first, developing also beside taller peas that grow fast from early May.

This is a wonderful combination. The turnips and radish grow strongly in cool spring weather and mature before potato leaves grow too large. Multi-sow radish and turnips, placing 5 seeds per cell for a four-plant clump. They can be transplanted around the middle of March, which could be at the same time as planting seed potatoes in mild areas. Your last frost date governs when to plant seed potatoes. I put them in the ground about a month beforehand; they will gain roots but very little new growth will appear at a time there might be a last frost. Radishes can even be direct sown in early March if fleece is placed over them. Peas are transplanted out in the middle of March and need sticks for support.

GROWING TIP

Use a protective covering of fleece across all these crops for the first month, usually until the peas become too tall. Then fold the fleece back to allow them growing height. I keep fleece over the radish and turnips until harvest, as a defence against cabbage root fly.

CULTIVARS

TURNIP See p.59.

RADISH See p.77.

POTATO

'Charlotte' Second early with slightly waxy tubers of great flavour.

'Jazzy' Second early with very waxy smooth tubers.

'Red Duke of York' First early cultivar, but I grow it as a second early, harvesting in early July. Floury red-skinned tubers, tasty and with good yields.

'Setanta' Maincrop potato with red-skinned, quite floury tubers of good flavour.

PEA See also p.91.

'Hurst Green Shaft' Pods bearing up to 10 sweet-tasting peas. Height 1.2m (4ft).

'Rondo' Good crops of large round pods containing up to 10 peas. Height 1m (3ft).

'Oregon Sugar Pod' A sweet mangetout, best picked thin; 1.2m (4ft).

KEY INFORMATION

TURNIP See p.59.

RADISH

Seed to harvest: 8–10 weeks **Seed to transplanting:** 3–4 weeks **Position:** Sun or part shade **Spacing:** 22cm (8½in) between rows, 3–5cm (1¼–2in) between each radish **Hardiness:** Moderately hardy

POTATO

Seed to harvest: 11 weeks (first early), 12 weeks (second early), 16 weeks (maincrop) **Position:** Full sun **Spacing:** 45–50cm (18–20in) **Hardiness:** Not frost hardy

PEA

Seed to harvest: 12–14 weeks **Seed to transplanting:** 3 weeks **Position:** Sun or part shade **Spacing:** 10cm (4in) apart within rows, 50cm (20in) between rows **Hardiness:** Hardy to –5°C (23°F)

TIMINGS

TURNIP

Sowing: Multi-sown mid-to late February (under cover) **Transplanting:** Mid-March **Harvesting:** Late April to May

RADISH

Sowing: Multi-sown mid-to late February (under cover; direct sow early March) **Transplanting:** Mid-March **Harvesting:** Late April to mid-May

POTATO

Planting seed potatoes: Early to mid-April (second earlies and maincrop potatoes) **Harvesting:** Late June to mid-July (second earlies); August (maincrop)

PEA

Sowing: Early March (under cover) **Transplanting:** Late March **Harvesting:** June to early July

SWEETCORN *between* WINTER SQUASH

COMPANION TYPE: OVERLAP (11–16 weeks), INTERPLANTING

The classic "three sisters" (sweetcorn, beans, and squash) is probably the best-known companion planting combination for vegetables. It was developed by native Americans for dry harvests and is less suitable for cooler UK conditions, so I grow corn for fresh harvest, between winter squash.

My adjustment for the UK climate is to leave out the beans and to plant corn for sweetcorn (rather than dry corn as in the three sisters), positioned between winter squash – the two crops fit together so nicely. There is enough room for one or two corn plants between each squash. It is often said that you should grow sweetcorn in a block, yet wind pollination still happens, producing well-filled cobs that are usually ready for harvest before the squash. You can take advantage of a warm May by direct sowing sweetcorn, placing 2 seeds per hole, thinning to the strongest plant.

GROWING TIP

As both crops enjoy warm conditions, use fleece to cover them if the first weeks after planting are cool, until warm weather is forecast.

CULTIVARS

SWEETCORN

'Earlibird' F1 Supersweet with small cobs; harvest from early August.

'Incredible' F1 Midseason cultivar with really tasty cobs, ready in late August.

'Tramunt' Open-pollinated, midseason selection with decent-sized cobs by September.

WINTER SQUASH

'Crown Prince' F1 Widely esteemed for its sweet flavour, dense texture, and excellent keeping qualities until May or longer, with silver-grey skin and dark orange flesh.

'Marina di Chioggia' Dark green, blistered, impressive fruits with excellent flavour.

'Uchiki Kuri' Orange-skinned, onion-shaped fruit with delicious chestnut flavour. Ripens early so it's suited to a temperate climate of cooler summers. Stores until early spring.

Note: Butternut squash need a long time to mature and are often a disappointment in temperate climates, unless it's an especially hot summer.

KEY INFORMATION

SWEETCORN

Seed to harvest: 13–19 weeks **Seed to transplanting:** 3–4 weeks **Position:** Full sun **Spacing:** 1m (3ft) **Hardiness:** Tender

WINTER SQUASH

Seed to harvest: 18–24 weeks **Seed to transplanting:** 4 weeks **Position:** Full sun **Spacing:** 1m (3ft) **Hardiness:** Tender

TIMINGS

SWEETCORN

Sowing: Late April to early May (under cover) **Transplanting:** Mid-May to early June (under fleece if it's cool) **Harvesting:** Early August to September

WINTER SQUASH

Sowing: Mid-April (under cover) **Transplanting:** First half of May (under fleece if it's cool) **Harvesting:** September to October

Overleaf: Squash 'Uchiki Kuri' growing with sweetcorn planted between and almost ready, late August (left). 'Crown Prince' squash in September, from two plants set between turnips in early May (right).

WINTER SQUASH *between* TURNIP

COMPANION TYPE: OVERLAP (1–4 weeks)

In temperate climates, winter squashes need as much time in the ground as possible. If you don't have space at planting time, I've found you can overlap them with early sowings of turnips, which allows the squash to establish while the turnips are reaching maturity.

Winter squash are a fantastic resource as they store for months, until April or May. This planting offers just a brief overlap, but provides an extra option for getting your squash into the ground on time, important in cooler climates and if you have limited space. Turnips are transplanted on the square in mid-March, and covered with fleece (see Growing Tip). They will be ready for a first harvest in late April.

Meanwhile, sow seed of winter squash under cover, a month before the last frost date. Take the first turnip harvests from the middle of the bed, providing space to transplant the squash, in early May. The spacing will look generous at 1m (3ft), but the squash plants fill this quickly, and more. Continue harvesting turnips until around 25 May, before they start to grow woody. In autumn, a light frost will not damage the thick-skinned squash, but it will kill the plants. Harvest squash by cutting the slender plant stems attached to it.

ALTERNATIVE CHOICES

Swap winter squash for courgettes, planted at a similar spacing in the centre of the bed.

CULTIVARS

WINTER SQUASH See p.63.

TURNIP See p.59.

KEY INFORMATION

WINTER SQUASH See p.63.

TURNIP See p.59.

TIMINGS

WINTER SQUASH

Sowing: 10–20 April (under cover) **Transplanting:** First half of May (best planted under fleece) **Harvesting:** September to October

TURNIP

Sowing: Mid-February (under cover) **Transplanting:** Mid-March (best planted under fleece) **Harvesting:** Late April to late May

---

GROWING TIP

Fleece adds double value here. Used over turnips it provides warmth for an early crop, then in April and May it protects against cabbage root fly. It also provides warmth for the winter squash when you plant them out in May, when conditions can still be cool. It can stay in place until the weather warms up.

DWARF FRENCH MARIGOLD
at the ends of beds

COMPANION TYPE: BONUS

This is a form of companion planting, with dwarf French marigolds (*Tagetes patula*) grown as transplants at the ends of my beds, rather than between plants. Here their beauty and colour are more visible and they require little extra space.

I grow French marigolds more than any other flower. They are compact in size, viable close to almost all vegetables, and bloom all summer even if you don't get round to deadheading from July. The plants tolerate dry weather, which keeps them smaller, and importantly, they do not self-seed to become a weed, unlike pot marigold (*Calendula officinalis*).

I sow in seed trays and prick out at the two-leaf stage into module cells. You can plant out after three weeks, or if the weather is cool, pot on into a 7cm (2¾in) pot and plant after another month. In dry summers I water them a little, and they access moisture from nearby vegetables, which are also watered. Saving seed works well, and after several years my own selection is larger and super-vigorous.

ALTERNATIVE CHOICES

Choose compact flowers that do not self-seed excessively. I favour dwarf nasturtiums such as *Tropaeolum majus* 'Empress of India' whose red blooms and dark leaves are great in salads. Consider *Dianthus*, cornflowers (*Centaurea cyanus*), smaller *Zinnia*, and *Malope trifida* 'Vulcan'.

Dwarf French marigolds with celery behind, in July.

CULTIVARS

FRENCH MARIGOLD (*Tagetes patula*)

Boy O Boy Series, mixed Compact, uniform plants with double flowers in orange, yellow, and dark red. 30cm (12in).

'Burning Embers' Deep red single flowers, each petal outlined in orange. 40–50cm (16–20in). Too large for polytunnel planting.

'Striped Marvel' Also sold as 'Harlequin', single flowers with petals striped red and yellow. 60cm (24in), so less suitable for small spaces.

KEY INFORMATION

FRENCH MARIGOLD

Seed to flowering: 7–8 weeks **Seed to transplanting:** 4–8 weeks **Position:** Full sun **Spacing:** 20–25cm (8–10in) **Hardiness:** Frost tender

TIMINGS

FRENCH MARIGOLD

Sowing: Mid-April to early June (ideal early May, under cover) **Transplanting:** Mid-May to early July (ideal early June) **Flowering:** June until the frosts

Overleaf: I'm picking courgettes on 9 July, and under the fleece is newly planted celery after broad beans have finished.

CARROT *between* LETTUCE

COMPANION TYPE: OVERLAP (4–6 weeks)

A combination I've had strong success with; carrots sown between rows of lettuce, which I harvest for individual leaves. Lettuce needs plenty of watering by summer, which provides carrots with moisture, while regular cropping of lettuce leaves keeps slug numbers down.

This pairing works nicely when you are cropping outer leaves of lettuce once a week or more (as opposed to cutting the whole head). Lettuces are planted in rows during early spring and will have been cropping for 4–6 weeks by the time you sow carrots in late May to June. Picking the outer leaves reduces slug numbers in two ways: harvests are older leaves, which is what slugs most like to eat, and you'll often remove a slug or two with harvested leaves. What remains is slug-free.

How to sow your carrots

Draw drills in the surface compost, using a wooden dibber, trowel, or even your fingers. Nantes-type carrots have great flavour and yield, and there are many cultivar options. In dry conditions, run water along the bottom of the drill before you drop seeds in. Carrots germinate easily in summer and appear after 10 days. Once the seedlings emerge you will have harvested more lettuce leaves, maintaining space for the carrot seedlings; lettuce harvests continue for 2–6 weeks, depending on variety. Usually, I twist out the lettuce before the middle of July. This combination would make a useful and productive choice for smaller spaces and could work with some light shade.

If the soil is dry, water the base of the carrot drills before sowing seed.

CULTIVARS

CARROT

Early cultivars are fast growing and sowings in early summer ensure quick germination. Maincrop cultivars harvest later.

'Berlicum' Large maincrop variant of Nantes, which has roots with rounded ends. Good for late harvests in October, but may need a mesh cover against root fly.

'Nantes Milan 2' Sweet, quick-growing early carrot with rounded cylindrical roots.

'Norwich' F1 Second early Nantes carrot, vigorous with good flavour.

LETTUCE

'Saragossa' A Batavian type with bronzed and rounded leaves and fantastic firm texture.

'Parris Island Cos' Vigorous, dark green cos with long, quite thick leaves of fine flavour.

'Oakus' and **'Navara'** Red oakleaf types that crop for a long period before bolting, but grow more slowly than green cultivars.

KEY INFORMATION

CARROT

Seed to harvest: 10–16 weeks **Position:** Sun or part shade **Spacing:** 1 carrot per 1cm (½in), 22cm (8½in) between rows **Hardiness:** Fully hardy

LETTUCE

Seed to harvest: 10–16 weeks **Position:** Sun or part shade; sun results in fewer slugs **Spacing:** 20cm (8in) in the rows and 30cm (12in) between rows **Hardiness:** Half hardy to hardy

TIMINGS

CARROT

Sowing: 25 May–10 July **Harvesting:** From 10 weeks after sowing

LETTUCE

Sowing: 20 February–10 March, transplant before early April **Harvesting:** Early May to mid-July

---

GROWING TIP

Don't leave more than a week between harvests of lettuce leaves. I find plants get too big and suck up the moisture, affecting the development of my carrots.

Harvesting lettuce outer leaves, between carrots I intersowed seven weeks earlier.

RADISH *intersown with* CARROT

COMPANION TYPE: CATCH CROP

If you are sowing a crop of carrots anyway, dropping a few radish seeds into the same drill uses no extra space for a second crop. Radishes come up within a week and mark your rows, allowing you to hand weed or hoe with confidence in the space between each row.

For an early harvest, I direct sow carrot seeds in the second half of March, certainly before 10 April, choosing an early selection. The radishes are tender, mild, and juicy grown at this cool time of year, more pungent if sown later. Add only a few radish seeds in each line, or their leaves grow thickly and weaken the carrots. Within a few weeks the radishes mature – the carrots are small, but then grow rapidly. It's not difficult to twist and ease out each radish without disturbing the well-rooted carrots. I recommend you cover sowings with fleece, to warm the bed and protect radishes from flea beetles and cabbage root fly. It also helps deter rabbits. After the radish harvest I replace the fleece with mesh, to protect carrots against root flies in late spring to early summer.

GROWING TIP

This combination works very well if you have compost mulched a bed a month or more before sowing, because germination is then more rapid and weeds much easier to pull out. Weed growth is likely under the fleece, out of sight, so remember to remove weeds after you roll the fleece back temporarily, after about three weeks.

CULTIVARS

RADISH

These are the two I grow, and you could sow a mix of both for an early and later radish harvest.

'French Breakfast' An old favourite with cylindrical red and white roots. Harvest early before the roots grow big and hollow.

'Rudi' Superb round red roots that can grow large without going soft or woody.

CARROT

'Amsterdam Forcing 3' Tasty, early-cropping selection for long, thin carrots.

'Nantes Milan 2' Sweet, quick-growing, early carrot with rounded cylindrical roots.

'Norwich' F1 Second early Nantes-type carrot with good flavour and vigour.

KEY INFORMATION

RADISH

Seed to harvest: 5–8 weeks **Position:** Sun or part shade **Spacing:** 22cm (8½in) between rows, 3–5cm (1¼–2in) between each radish **Hardiness:** Moderately hardy

CARROT See page 35.

'Rudi' radish harvest in late April from a sowing with carrots six weeks earlier.

TIMINGS

RADISH

Direct sowing: Mid-March to early April (at the same time as the carrots)
Harvesting: Late April to mid-May

CARROT

Direct sowing: Mid-March to early April (at the same time as the radish)
Harvesting: 10–13 weeks after sowing

BEETROOT *between* ONION

COMPANION TYPE: OVERLAP (4–5 weeks)

Maincrop bulb onions finish growing and are cleared in mid- to late summer, when recently transplanted beetroot will have both the space and time needed to grow large before winter.

You need to be creative when finding spaces between the quite large onion plants, in order to slot in three-week-old beetroot transplants at the end of June. Initially these may be covered by onion leaves, and establish invisibly while the onions mature for a further 3–5 weeks, depending on the cultivar. Usually they are ready for harvesting before late July. A gentle twist frees the onions, leaving their roots in the soil. The beetroot plants are now established and quickly cover the newly available space with their rapidly expanding leaves.

ALTERNATIVE CHOICES

Autumn salads work well between onions; for example, endive, chicory, or lettuce sown in the second week of June can be transplanted in early July between red onions (these mature later than white or yellow). The onions are harvested at the end of July, and the salad leaves crop until November.

CULTIVARS

BEETROOT

'Burpee's Golden' Yellow flesh and a sweet, less earthy taste than some yellow beets.

'Cheltenham Green Top' Green leaved with long roots and really good flavour.

'Robuschka' Vigorous with dark red roots, good for December harvests and then it stores well.

ONION

Maincrop bulb onions can be grown as sets, or from seed as multi-sow onions, 3 to 4 in a clump.

'Red Baron' Deep red onion, either from seed or sets. Stores well.

'Rose de Roscoff' Rose-tinted, rapidly maturing onion, harvesting in early July.

'Sturon' Old cultivar with yellow flesh and fine yields of rounded bulbs. Stores well.

KEY INFORMATION

BEETROOT

Seed to harvest: 14–20 weeks **Seed to transplanting:** 3–4 weeks **Position:** Sun or part shade **Spacing:** 25–30cm (10–12in) between multi-sown clumps
Hardiness: Hardy

ONION

Seed to harvest: 20 weeks (up to 24 for red onions), sets to harvest 17 weeks **Seed to transplanting:** 4–5 weeks **Position:** Sun **Spacing:** 25–30cm (10–12in) between multi-sown clumps, or plant sets in rows across the bed, 10–15cm (4–6in) between onion sets, rows 30cm (12in) apart
Hardiness: Hardy

TIMINGS

BEETROOT

Sowing: Early June (under cover)
Transplanting: Mid- to late June (around the summer solstice) **Harvesting:** September to early December

ONION

Sowing: 20 February to early March (under cover) **Transplanting:** End March to early April **Harvesting:** Mid-July to early August (depending on cultivar)

BROCCOLI *with interplanted* BEETROOT

COMPANION TYPE: INTERPLANTING

I found this successful after summer slugs ate four of my nine purple sprouting broccoli plants. There is not usually enough space to transplant beetroot between broccoli, but it's an example of turning a problem into an opportunity!

Interplanting allows you to make use of unexpected spaces, here provided by the slugs. Purple and white sprouting broccoli grow through winter to crop in spring, and summer planting works well for both crops. I enjoyed a 1.3kg (3lb) harvest of beetroot in autumn and winter, while the five remaining broccoli plants filled the space, growing larger than usual and giving a bumper harvest. Having "spares" available is important, because transplanting beetroot in mid-July is too late for sowing, but I had plants ready that I could call on. I find beetroot will hold in module cells for 4–5 weeks from when it is sown.

GROWING TIP

Watch out for slugs and flea beetles, insects that eat small holes in broccoli leaves. Sowing plants under cover helps, as does covering new plantings with mesh on hoops. Through autumn I remove lower leaves to reduce slug food and habitat. Bird netting is often needed in winter and spring.

CULTIVARS

BROCCOLI

'Claret' F1 My go-to purple sprouting, a modern hybrid producing a large central head, then side shoots over many weeks.

'Rudolph' F1 Purple sprouting broccoli that crops from midwinter in mild weather, but the harvest is less than from spring broccoli cultivars.

'White Eye' White sprouting broccoli cropping from late winter with tender, great-tasting spears.

BEETROOT See p.79.

TIMINGS

BROCCOLI

Sowing: Early to mid-June (under cover)
Transplanting: Early to mid-July
Harvesting: March to April

BEETROOT

Sowing: Early June (under cover)
Transplanting: Early July
Harvesting: November

KEY INFORMATION

BROCCOLI (Purple or white sprouting)

Seed to harvest: 30–42 weeks according to season and cultivar **Seed to transplanting:** 3–5 weeks **Position:** Sun, but tolerates some shade **Spacing:** 50–60cm (20–24in) **Hardiness:** Hardy

BEETROOT

Seed to harvest: 22–24 weeks **Seed to transplanting:** 2–5 weeks **Position:** Sun or semi-shade **Spacing:** 25–30cm (10–12in) between multi-sown clumps **Hardiness:** Hardy

Beetroot interplanted after other broccoli had been eaten by slugs.

BEETROOT *between* GARLIC

COMPANION TYPE: OVERLAP (4–6 weeks)

Garlic suits overlap plantings because its foliage casts little shade, and it is cropped early in the season, giving opportunities to experiment with plantings. Beetroot is an easy-to-raise companion, and it can crop a month after the garlic has been removed, or later for large beetroot.

This combination proves easier when, the previous October, you planted garlic in 25–30cm (10–12in) rows across rather than along a bed, allowing easy access to sow, plant, and weed between rows. Either sow beetroot direct in the soil, in rows between garlic in early April, or pop in multi-sown module plants in late April. Another option is to scatter carrot seed between garlic plants about a month before you harvest. You could also transplant celeriac or lettuce between garlic in mid-May.

CULTIVARS

BEETROOT See p.53.

GARLIC

Both softneck and hardneck cultivars are suitable for interplanting. Softneck garlics grow bigger bulbs with smaller, more pungent cloves; hardnecks mature around three weeks later and cloves are easier to peel.

'Doocot' Hardneck cultivar good for cooler conditions with some resistance to rust.

'Provence Wight' Softneck early garlic with large bulbs and plump cloves.

'Solent Wight' Softneck late garlic with small white bulbs ready for harvesting in early July.

KEY INFORMATION

BEETROOT See p.53.

GARLIC

Planting to harvest: 32 weeks **Position:** Sun **Spacing:** 30cm (12in) between rows, 10cm (4in) between each clove **Hardiness:** Hardy

Four weeks after transplanting beetroot between garlic, late May. See the same beetroot in early September on p.15.

TIMINGS

BEETROOT

Sowing: Early April (direct or to raise transplants) **Transplanting:** Mid-April to May **Harvesting:** July onwards

GARLIC

Planting: (From cloves) mid-October **Harvesting:** 10–20 June (softneck), early July (hardneck)

GROWING TIP

Orange pustules on garlic leaves indicate rust. Plants will tolerate mild infections but if leaves become covered, harvest bulbs right away. Reduce rust by growing garlic under cover (see p.133); rain in early spring speeds the development of rust.

SAVOY CABBAGE *between* ONION

COMPANION TYPE: OVERLAP (3–5 weeks)

This combination has always worked well for me and makes a good alternative to using beetroot between maincrop bulb onions (see p.79). Spacing will be irregular, cabbages popped in where you find a decent gap between the swelling clumps of multi-sown onions, or between onions from sets.

I discovered this pairing when I had no space for a tray of Savoy cabbages one hot July. It was hard work to make holes in the dry soil between onions, but the cabbage root balls were small, planted from 3cm (1¼in) module cells. Don't worry about planting the cabbages in rows; they can be dotted around. Look for gaps with a minimum of 40cm (16in) between plants. Water each cabbage individually, because onions ripen better when soil is dry. Then after 2–3 weeks gently twist out the onions to remove them. You may have to net the cabbage against insects and/or pigeons.

ALTERNATIVE CHOICES

Try a quick-growing ball-head cabbage such as 'Golden Acre'. The timings for sowing and transplanting are the same, but they can mature faster, in 12 weeks, by October. If cabbages don't appeal, you could also transplant beetroot, kale, lettuce, and herbs such as coriander and parsley.

CULTIVARS

SAVOY CABBAGE

'Cantasa' F1 An early cultivar forming good uniform heads, maturing in November.

'Ormskirk Late' Open-pollinated, producing more outer leaves than heart.

'Vertus' Late-cropping, hardy Savoy cabbage with flattish heads and a mild, not-too-bitter flavour.

ONION See p.79.

KEY INFORMATION

SAVOY CABBAGE

Seed to harvest: 22–36 weeks depending on cultivar **Seed to transplanting:** 3–4 weeks **Position:** Sun or part shade **Spacing:** 40–50cm (16–20in) **Hardiness:** Hardy

ONION See p.79.

TIMINGS

SAVOY CABBAGE

Sowing: Second half of June (under cover, I aim for 20 June) **Transplanting:** Early July **Harvesting:** November to March (depending on cultivar)

ONION See p.79.

Late July onion bed with Savoy cabbage transplanted between.

FENNEL *between* RIDGE CUCUMBER

COMPANION TYPE: OVERLAP (3–4 weeks)

This appealing late summer combination teams highly productive outdoor ridge cucumbers, which cover the ground through summer's second half, with delicious Florence fennel that can be harvested successfully in autumn. I find the biggest challenge is finding space to slot in fennel plants amid the cucumber foliage.

Florence fennel in a temperate climate has two possible dates for sowing; in spring for early summer harvests or, as here, in July for harvests in late autumn. The sowing date is quite precise; I favour 20 July, and mid-July works well. If you sow too early the fennel bolts; too late and cold weather can prevent full maturity. Transplanting is in mid-August, when space is hard to find. A few years ago, I dared to pop them between ridge cucumber plants, which looked almost impossible, but after trimming off old and diseased leaves there was just enough room. Use a dibber to make holes for each fennel root ball and water them well as the thirsty cucumbers will rob some of the water. You may need to clear more of the older, slightly mildewed cucumber leaves to aid development.

Removing the cucumbers

The cucumbers continue cropping until around 10 September, by which time powdery mildew is covering many leaves. Now is the time to bid adieu to them (see Growing Tip). Suddenly visible, the fennel grows away strongly. Plants bulb up fast, so the first harvest can be six weeks after removing the cucumbers. See p.48 for a fennel harvest in late spring to early summer.

By late August the fennel are strong plants, while cucumber leaves have more mildew.

GROWING TIP

To harvest a cucumber, cut the main stem off just above the roots, leaving the root ball in situ to help feed soil microbes. Compost the rest of the plant and don't worry about mildew or other disease. I never experience problems with composting similar material.

CULTIVARS

FLORENCE FENNEL

'Perfektion' A favourite of mine, as it gives excellent results in both June and October.

'Rondo' F1 Quick growing and easily obtained.

'Zefa Fino' Fast-growing and good for early or late sowings.

RIDGE CUCUMBER

'La Diva' F1 Compact plant producing good crops of crisp cucumbers 12cm (5in) long.

'Marketmore' Great flavour with 20cm (8in) fruits with notable spines, so peel before eating.

'Tanja' Slender, spine-free fruit, 35cm (14in) long, in profusion. Refreshing flavour.

KEY INFORMATION

FLORENCE FENNEL

Seed to harvest: 11–15 weeks **Seed to transplanting:** 3–5 weeks **Position:** Sun or part shade **Spacing:** 30cm (12in) **Hardiness:** Hardy to −2°C (28°F)

RIDGE CUCUMBER

Seed to harvest: 11 weeks **Seed to transplanting:** 3–4 weeks **Position:** Full sun **Spacing:** 60cm (24in) in the row and 1m (3ft) either side **Hardiness:** Frost tender

TIMINGS

FLORENCE FENNEL

Sowing: Third week of July **Transplanting:** Mid-August **Harvesting:** Mid-October to mid-November

RIDGE CUCUMBER

Sowing: Early to mid-May under cover, or direct sow early to mid-June
Transplanting: Late May to early June
Harvesting: Mid-July to September

Final harvest of 'Tanja' cucumber in early September before removing the plants. The fennel is now looking strong.

RIDGE CUCUMBER *between* STRAWBERRY *and* PEA

COMPANION TYPE: OVERLAP (4–6 weeks)

This idea makes best use of a quite small gap between existing crops. A couple of outdoor ridge cucumber plants can be slotted into the limited space between rows of peas and strawberries that will finish cropping around four weeks later.

Allow about 1m (3ft) between the two existing crops. Because cucumbers are so tender, I usually lay a cover of fleece on top for the first three or four weeks. The peas (around 10 plants) are positioned in a row across the 1.2m (4ft) bed, 60cm (24in) from the strawberries, and given support. They finish by the end of June. The strawberries finish in early July, when we cut leaves and stems to 2.5–4cm (1–1½in) above ground level, which removes any runners and allows regrowth from the base. The timings work nicely; I've found that by mid-July, the cucumber plants can produce up to 1kg (2lb 3oz) of fruit. This space-efficient combination is good for smaller plots, and you could scale it down to just a single cucumber plant, if you wish.

ALTERNATIVE CHOICES

Swap cucumbers for courgettes or tomatoes, both of which have similar timings and don't need too much space in the first weeks after planting. Instead of peas, you could grow carrots or broad beans.

CULTIVARS

RIDGE CUCUMBER See p.88.

STRAWBERRY

'Cambridge Favourite' Medium-sized, tasty fruits mid-season.

'Florence' Late-season selection bearing large dark red fruits.

'Marshmello' I particularly recommend this as it finishes cropping sooner than many others, with excellent flavour.

PEA

I avoid tall selections that mean too much moisture competition for neighbouring plants.

'Feltham First' Early-cropping, short selection, pods containing 8 peas. Height 50cm (20in).

'Hurst Green Shaft' Pods bearing up to 10 sweet-tasting peas. Height 1.2m (4ft).

'Rondo' Good crops of large round pods containing up to 10 peas. Height 1m (3ft).

KEY INFORMATION

RIDGE CUCUMBER See p.88.

STRAWBERRY

Planting to harvest: Perennial, so grows from year to year **Position:** Sun or part shade **Spacing:** 30cm (12in) **Hardiness:** Hardy

PEA See p.61.

Fleece over the cucumber plants in early June is helping them to establish, close to peas and strawberries.

TIMINGS

RIDGE CUCUMBER

Sowing: Early to mid-May under cover, or direct sow early to mid-June
Transplanting: Late May to early June
Harvesting: Mid-July to mid-September

STRAWBERRY

Planting: July to September; I keep plants for 3–5 years until cropping is much less
Harvesting: Early June to mid-July

PEA

Sowing: Early March (under cover) or mid-March direct **Transplanting:** Late March
Harvesting: June

RIDGE CUCUMBER *between* POTATO *and* BEETROOT

COMPANION TYPE: INTERPLANTING, OVERLAP (4 weeks)

This pleasing combination makes great use of available space. The outdoor ridge cucumbers are transplanted or direct sown and gradually establish while neighbouring crops of beetroot and first early potatoes mature.

The cucumbers don't need a lot of space at the beginning, but can quietly extend roots while much larger neighbouring plants are finishing. The beetroot and potatoes will be harvested within four or five weeks of the cucumber plants arriving. The small cucumber plants (or seed) slot between them, 30cm (12in) from the beetroot, 40cm (16in) from the base of the potatoes, which at this stage are growing quickly. You need just two cucumber plants across a 1.2m (4ft) wide bed, but I always grow extra in case one fails. Once the beetroot and potatoes are harvested in late June, the cucumbers explode into growth. I give them 1m (3ft) of space either side, which they quickly cover. They can be highly productive through July and August, especially with regular watering.

GROWING TIP

After I plant the cucumbers and water them in, I cover them lightly with fleece for a month. This allows the heat-loving cucumbers to establish more quickly, and also guards against occasional chilly nights.

CULTIVARS

RIDGE CUCUMBER See p.88.

POTATO (first earlies)

'Apache' Red skin and a buttery flavour; harvest young as it can grow until August as a maincrop.

'Casablanca' Good crops of large tubers; matures slightly later than other first earlies.

'Red Duke of York' Well-flavoured potato with red skin and pale flesh.

BEETROOT See p.53.

KEY INFORMATION

RIDGE CUCUMBER See p.88.

POTATO

Seed to harvest: 11 weeks **Position:** Sun or part shade **Spacing:** 45cm (18in) **Hardiness:** Frost tender

BEETROOT

Seed to harvest: 16 weeks **Seed to transplanting:** 3–4 weeks **Position:** Sun or part shade **Spacing:** 30cm (12in) between multi-sown clumps **Hardiness:** Hardy

TIMINGS

RIDGE CUCUMBER

Sowing: Early to mid-May under cover, or direct sow early June
Transplanting: Late May to early June
Harvesting: Mid-July to mid-September

POTATO (first earlies)

Planted: Mid-late March **Harvesting:** June

BEETROOT

Sowing: Multi-sow late February
Transplanting: Mid- to late March
Harvesting: Mid- to end June

By late June the potatoes and beetroot are soon to finish, with cucumbers now growing strongly.

SUMMER

DWARF FRENCH BEAN
between FENNEL

COMPANION TYPE: OVERLAP (4–5 weeks)

Florence fennel is such a protective and productive crop for combining with others, in this case sheltering delicate French bean plants while they are young. You can use tomatoes or outdoor ridge cucumbers instead of the beans, as both are planted out at a similar time of year.

The bed I grow this combination in is exposed to the prevailing south-west wind. Dwarf French beans have thin stems and do not thrive in windy conditions, but here the plants establish quickly, thanks to shelter from the fennel plants, whose feathery foliage protects them while casting little shade. I transplant or sow direct the French beans between the fennel, 3–4 weeks before the fennel bulbs swell for harvest. Harvest fennel by cutting below the bulbs, at or just below ground level so that there will be no regrowth. Then the space is available for the bean plants to grow. Their roots will explore the channels in the soil which become available as fennel roots decompose.

GROWING TIP

Keep a close eye on the fennel bulbs, even when small. They are inclined to elongate if plants move towards flowering, a sign you need to harvest because they will not swell any more.

CULTIVARS

DWARF FRENCH BEAN

'**Elba**' Fast-maturing, slim, smooth stringless beans to 15cm (6in) long.

'**Maxi**' Early-cropping selection with prolific, green, 20cm (8in) stringless pods.

'**Safari**' Prolific, vigorous selection for later crops of green pods 12cm (5in) long.

FLORENCE FENNEL See p.88.

KEY INFORMATION

DWARF FRENCH BEAN

Seed to harvest: 8–10 weeks **Seed to transplanting:** 2–3 weeks **Position:** Sun **Spacing:** 30cm (12in) **Hardiness:** Frost tender

FLORENCE FENNEL See p.88.

TIMINGS

DWARF FRENCH BEAN

Sowing: Early May (under cover) or mid-May direct **Transplanting:** Mid- to late May **Harvesting:** July to mid-August

FLORENCE FENNEL

Sowing: Late February (under cover with some heat) **Transplanting:** Late March **Harvesting:** June

In early June the fennel is ready to harvest, and the French beans will soon need the space.

CHARD *between* DWARF FRENCH BEAN

COMPANION TYPE: INTERPLANTING AND OVERLAP (8–9 weeks, for as long as the beans are growing)

This combination differs from many of my suggestions as you are transplanting one crop (beans) while direct sowing the other (chard) at the same time, ideally the beginning of July. The vibrant bean flowers and chard foliage provide colourful interplanting with a lengthy period of overlap.

Chard can be sown in mid-April for summer and autumn harvests, or as late as mid-July for plants that survive winter more strongly, for leaves the following spring. Sow two rows of chard in between three rows of dwarf French beans. Use a dibber and drop 2 chard seeds into each hole for 2–4 plants per clump. French beans are most generous in the first month of cropping, so don't leave them growing for too long. The chard is shaded at first, but soon grows as fast as the beans. About 10 weeks after transplanting, cut the bean plants off at ground level, leaving roots in to nourish the soil. The chard will respond with lush harvests into autumn, and possible survival through winter leading to welcome new leaves in spring, until they flower in May. I like red and orange stems, so I select plants with those stem colours for seeding in the following year.

Early September harvest of chard, between French bean plants that will soon finish cropping.

CULTIVARS

CHARD

'Bright Lights' and **'Rainbow'** Mixes of white-, orange-, yellow-, and red-stemmed plants.

'Bright Yellow' Green leaves with bright yellow stalks and leaf veins.

'White Silver' Swiss chard with broad, white stems, productive and hardier than more colourful selections.

DWARF FRENCH BEAN See p.95.

KEY INFORMATION

CHARD

Seed to harvest: 8–10 weeks **Position:** Sun or part shade **Spacing:** 30cm (12in) between clumps, 45cm (18in) between rows
Hardiness: Tolerates light frost

DWARF FRENCH BEAN See p.95.

TIMINGS

CHARD

Direct sowing: Late June to early July (and later) sowings can succeed **Harvesting:** September to November; plants may survive winter to provide spring crops

DWARF FRENCH BEAN

Sowing: Mid-June (under cover)
Transplanting: Late June to early July
Harvesting: Mid- to late August

GROWING TIP

Forgo an early chard harvest, then cut stems about 5cm (2in) above ground level when you clear away the beans. The new growth that emerges in September will be stronger, short, and sturdy, providing a welcome harvest through October and November, then a lot in spring before flowering in May.

French bean harvests were plentiful through late summer, and soon the chard will use all that space.

DWARF FRENCH BEAN *between* LETTUCE

COMPANION TYPE: OVERLAP (3–6 weeks)

A crop of dwarf French beans will establish while you are enjoying the final 3–4 weeks of harvesting outer lettuce leaves, which makes space for the new beans. Regular watering is important when growing lettuce, and this also helps young bean plants develop well.

I use a dibber to make holes between the lettuce and direct sow my French beans, although you can also use transplants. The lettuce can be 23–25cm (9–10in) apart. Timings depend partly on when you started your lettuce, and the idea is to sow French beans around six weeks before you think the lettuce will finish cropping, which for spring-planted lettuce could be the first week of July, depending on the cultivar; some, such as 'Saragossa', may continue until mid-July. Lettuce stems twist out easily, allowing all the space for bean plants, which are now fast growing.

CULTIVARS

DWARF FRENCH BEAN See p.95.
LETTUCE See p.115.
'Saragossa' Red Batavian lettuce forming a compact plant with a crunchy texture.

KEY INFORMATION

DWARF FRENCH BEAN See p.95.
LETTUCE See p.115.

TIMINGS

DWARF FRENCH BEAN
Sowing: No earlier than 20 May
Transplanting: Early to mid-June
Harvesting: Mid-July to August

LETTUCE
Sowing: Late February (under cover)
Transplanting: Late March to early April
Harvesting: Late April to early July

Lettuce are close to final harvest, with French bean plants well established.

ALTERNATIVE CHOICES

Swap the French beans for tomatoes or other crops that may be planted out at the same time, such as spring onions or beetroot. You can also direct sow carrots between lettuce (see p.72).

SPINACH *under* CORDON TOMATO

COMPANION TYPE: OVERLAP (7–9 weeks)

This perfectly timed planting pairs the end of cordon or indeterminate tomatoes with the start of long-season spinach, which slots in neatly under tomato plants that are now growing less strongly. After winter you will enjoy increasingly large spinach leaves from March to early May, all from one August sowing.

Spinach shows quality and longevity from late-summer sowings. Its summer flowering season is finished and so plants turn their energy to leaf growth for many months, until rising to flower the following May and June. I pinch out the tips, or "stop" my outdoor cordon tomatoes in late July (if growing under cover I do this in mid-August), by pinching out the growing tips. I remove lower tomato leaves to open up space below. By August you can have 45cm (18in) of clear stem, with lower trusses still ripening – sufficient light and space for spinach. The soil will be dry, so I water a little before dibbing holes and popping in spinach seeds or transplants. They grow slowly until the tomatoes finish, usually in early October.

GROWING TIPS

Water spinach as little as possible in the first few weeks. Drier soil now will hasten final ripening of the tomatoes. In winter, older spinach leaves turn yellow and attract slugs. I remove those leaves to compost, which makes it easier to pick the new leaves from mid-February.

Mid-September, 12 days after transplanting spinach under tomatoes.

Removing the tomatoes

Remaining fruit may be used green in chutney, while any with colour can be bought indoors to finish ripening. Once picking is complete, cut around and remove the tomato stems, leaving most of the roots in the ground to feed the soil. Now there is free soil, space, and light for the spinach to grow strongly. Spinach tolerates dark and cool better than many other plants, so mild autumns may provide you with small harvests in November, and with winter cold, the leaves become particularly sweet, because they use sugars like antifreeze to reduce frost damage.

CULTIVARS

SPINACH

'Giant Winter' Fast growing with large leaves; starts to flower from mid-April.

'Medania' My favourite as it is winter hardy, long-lived, and the dark green leaves are tasty in salads. Crops well until early June.

'Missouri' F1 and **'Emilia' F1** Large dark green leaves, quicker to crop than 'Medania'.

CORDON TOMATO See p.39.

'Rose Crush' F1 Good yields of large and crimson-red beef tomatoes, with dense flesh and a full flavour.

KEY INFORMATION

SPINACH

Seed to harvest: 6–8 weeks **Seed to transplanting:** 2–4 weeks **Position:** Full sun or part shade **Spacing:** 20–25cm (8–10in) **Hardiness:** Hardy to −15°C (5°F), perhaps colder

CORDON TOMATO See p.39.

TIMINGS

SPINACH

Sowing: Early to mid-August (direct sow, or raise transplants under cover) **Transplanting:** mid- to late August **Harvesting:** October to May

CORDON TOMATO

Sowing: Mid-March (under cover) **Transplanting:** Early May (under cover) to late May (outdoors) **Harvesting:** July to mid-October

SPINACH *between* LETTUCE

COMPANION TYPE: OVERLAP (3–6 weeks)

This overlap combination illustrates the incredible growth speed of spinach transplants in late summer and early autumn. When they go in between much larger lettuce they look so small but, within one month, the roles are reversed and spinach is dominant.

The lettuce, which is picked for its outer leaves, has been cropping since mid-July after being transplanted in late June. The spinach can go in between the lettuce as tiny transplants just 16 days after sowing, from mid-August. The lettuce crops for another 4–6 weeks, depending on cultivar, while spinach soon overtakes the lettuce in size. You then twist out the lettuce plants, leaving a bed of spinach that will crop in October and November, and often overwinter. Sometimes I spread a little compost between spinach plants in December, when they are small. Otherwise, 2–3cm (¾–1¼in) compost goes on in May, before planting the next vegetable.

CULTIVARS

SPINACH See p.104.
LETTUCE See p.115.

KEY INFORMATION

SPINACH See p.104.
LETTUCE See p.115.

TIMINGS

SPINACH
Sowing: Early August (under cover)
Transplanting: Mid- to late August
Harvesting: Late September to early May

LETTUCE
Sowing: Late May to early June (under cover)
Transplanting: Mid- to late June
Harvesting: Mid-July to late September (depending on cultivar)

PARSNIP *intersown between* SPINACH

COMPANION TYPE: OVERLAP (4–6 weeks)

The beauty of this combination is that the moist soil around spring-sown spinach, which we often need to water, helps ensure good germination of parsnip seed. Regular harvests of leaves allow space to sow parsnips in rows between the spinach plants, and they emerge while you continue to pick spinach.

I can sow parsnips at any time from March to June here, but later sowings perform really well and give roots that suffer less canker disease. Parsnip seedlings take 2 weeks or more to emerge, and continual moisture is necessary for germination. The spinach is multi-sown under cover in late winter, 3 seeds in each cell to provide at least two seedlings, for planting in early spring. Cover young plants with fleece, and the outer leaves can be harvested from late April. Sow parsnips any time from then. Use a wooden dibber to draw a 2cm (¾in) deep line, water in the line if conditions are dry, then drop parsnip seed in. Spinach flowers from early June and when plants are twisted out, there is more space for parsnips. You could also direct sow carrots or beetroot between rows of spinach, using the same timings.

Sowing parsnips between spinach in May.

CULTIVARS

PARSNIP

'Gladiator' F1 A real winner, a strong-growing selection with long, evenly tapering roots, and some canker resistance.

'Javelin' F1 Fine selection with roots even longer than 'Gladiator'.

'White Gem' Good old-fashioned cultivar, the roots have broad shoulders and good flavour.

SPINACH See p.104.

KEY INFORMATION

PARSNIP

Seed to harvest: 22 weeks **Position:** Sun or part shade **Spacing:** Rows 30cm (12in) apart, 1 seed per 1cm (½in) thinned to 2cm (¾in) **Hardiness:** Hardy to at least −15°C (5°F)

SPINACH See p.104.

TIMINGS

PARSNIP

Direct sowing: Late April to May
Harvesting: Mid-October to March

SPINACH

Sowing: Mid-February to early March (under cover) **Transplanting:** Mid- to late March
Harvesting: Late April to early June

GROWING TIP

Spinach likes moist, rich soil and needs to be direct sown or transplanted into soil with a decent mulch for compost, to ensure a better harvest. I spread compost at Christmas to keep the soil covered through winter, and to ensure a soft surface for sowing parsnips.

PARSNIP *intersown between* LETTUCE

COMPANION TYPE: OVERLAP (6–7 weeks)

This is well worth trying if you are already growing rows of leaf lettuce. The parsnips require little effort except for moist soil while they germinate. Pick and water the lettuce as usual and before you know it, the parsnips are popping up.

This combination works nicely because lettuce needs plenty of moisture, which benefits the long period of parsnip seed germination. Lettuce leaves are harvested regularly, allowing space for the parsnips to be intersown in rows during the first half of May (see p.106). Parsnips are usefully slow-growing at first, so they don't get in the way of lettuce harvests, which can continue for up to seven weeks after sowing the parsnips. The lettuce will finish around the first week of July, depending on cultivar, and then their stems twist out easily. The parsnips will be ready to harvest from mid-October.

CULTIVARS

PARSNIP See p.108.
LETTUCE See p.115.

KEY INFORMATION

PARSNIP See p.108.
LETTUCE See p.115.

TIMINGS

PARSNIP
Direct sowing: Early to mid-May
Harvesting: Mid-October to March

LETTUCE
Sowing: Late February to early March (under cover) **Transplanting:** Late March to early April **Harvesting:** Late April to early July

DILL and CORIANDER under CORDON CUCUMBER

COMPANION TYPE: INTERPLANTING

This combination for a greenhouse or polytunnel uses the free space at the foot of mature cordon cucumbers that are trained up strings or netting and continue cropping higher up. The timing is perfect as late summer is also the best time to sow dill and coriander.

Cordon cucumbers, by the end of summer and once their lower leaves are cut off, have open space underneath where new plants can establish. The dill and coriander seedlings do not need large amounts of food and moisture and have a complementary pattern of growth. I prefer to transplant young plants of dill and coriander in the second or third week of August. (You can also direct sow the seeds in late July.) You can grow these herbs under tomatoes, too, under cover or outdoors.

GROWING TIPS

Remove lower leaves of your cucumber plants as they grow, providing space for the herbs. They often develop powdery mildew, so removing them helps maintain good hygiene and improves air flow. Cucumber plants need less water by September and in comparison, the herbs can be watered a little more.

CULTIVARS

DILL/CORIANDER

These herbs have similar growing requirements. While I have not noticed significant differences between the few selections of dill, coriander has more variety.

'Calypso' Compact, low-growing coriander that is slow to bolt.

'Confetti' Coriander selection with feathery, light green foliage.

'Cruiser' My go-to coriander, does not flower quickly and bears broad, dark green leaves.

'Domino' Compact dill variety with grey-blue leaves, and tasty seeds by late summer.

CORDON CUCUMBER

'Carmen' F1 My favourite, producing abundant fruit to 40cm (16in) long.

'Mini Munch' F1 Produces 8–10cm (3–4in) cucumbers.

'Passandra' F1 Abundant, half-size fruit around 15cm (6in).

KEY INFORMATION

DILL/CORIANDER

Seed to harvest: 6–7 weeks **Seed to transplanting:** 3 weeks **Position:** Sun or semi-shade **Spacing:** 15cm (6in) **Hardiness:** Stands moderate frost

CORDON CUCUMBER

Seed to harvest: 10 weeks **Seed to transplanting:** 4 weeks **Position:** Partly shaded greenhouse or polytunnel **Spacing:** 60cm (24in) **Hardiness:** Frost tender

TIMINGS

DILL/CORIANDER

Sowing: By early August; earlier and plants bolt, later and they are less productive
Transplanting: Mid- to late August
Harvesting: September to early October

CORDON CUCUMBER

Sowing: Mid-April **Transplanting:** Mid-May
Harvesting: July to early October

Overleaf: Dill forms a carpet of green under tall cucumber plants, with marigolds under the tomatoes (left). Pink celery is a good option for cutting and this is its regrowth, overshadowed by dahlias (right).

CELERY *between* LETTUCE

COMPANION TYPE: OVERLAP (4–8 weeks)

Overlapping transplants of celery with rapidly maturing lettuce, already being cropped for its succulent outer leaves, makes good use of space. Celery starts slowly as small transplants but if you keep it well watered, growth speeds up. For this combination, sow in April to transplant in May, for harvests from mid- to late summer. You can sow celery in March, in which case the lettuce need to finish by solstice.

This combination is similar to growing celeriac with lettuce (see p.46), but the celery can be sown and transplanted earlier than celeriac, in rows across the bed. Celery will not be in the way while you are picking the leaves of the lettuce from late April. I recommend quite close spacing of celery, to grow nice slender stalks with fewer side shoots, which diminish the size and quality of main stems. Initial growth is not rapid. Twist out the lettuce as or before it reaches flowering stage, usually by late June, to allow the celery to bulk up.

GROWING TIP

To succeed with celery keep it well watered, every two days in dry weather. Plants must have moisture at the root, which also benefits the lettuces.

CULTIVARS

CELERY

Chinese pink celery Unusual pink type to try for fun. The harvest is less generous, but you can pick the slender outer stems rather than crop the entire head, or cut all stems to 5cm (2in), up to three times.

'Tango' F1 Tall, pale green, "self-blanching" stems standing hot weather, and with some bolting resistance.

'Victoria' F1 Tasty, tender, dark green stalks, an easy and vigorous selection.

LETTUCE

Avoid Batavian lettuce types or any that will go on cropping for too long; ideally they should be removed by the end of June.

'Little Gem' Small cos grown for its heads, but also good for harvesting outer leaves.

'Oakus' and **'Navara'** Red oakleaf types which crop for a long period, but grow more slowly than green cultivars. Not too large, so good for growing with celery or celeriac.

'Parris Island Cos' Vigorous, dark green cos with long thick leaves of fine flavour.

KEY INFORMATION

CELERY

Seed to harvest: 20 weeks **Seed to transplanting:** 5–7 weeks **Position:** Stands some shade (which can blanch the stems a little) **Spacing:** Rows 30cm (12in) apart, plants 20cm (8in) within rows **Hardiness:** Stalks are damaged by moderate frost

LETTUCE

Seed to harvest: 8–10 weeks **Seed to transplanting:** 4–5 weeks **Position:** Sun or part shade **Spacing:** Rows 30cm (12in) apart, 20cm (8in) between each plant **Hardiness:** Hardy but won't stand regular frost

TIMINGS

CELERY

Sowing: March to April (under cover) **Transplanting:** Early May **Harvesting:** July to August

LETTUCE

Sowing: Late February (under cover) **Transplanting:** Late March to early April **Harvesting:** Late April to late June

SPRING ONION *between* KALE

COMPANION TYPE: OVERLAP (4–8 weeks), catch crop

This overlap planting makes the most of considerable free space between kale plants during the first weeks after planting to grow spring onions as a catch crop. Transplant multi-sown spring onions to fill the gaps until their harvest, by which time the kale will be using all the space.

This works in much the same way as the combination with beetroot (p.52). This time, planting is done later in the year and the accompanying kale are spaced wide, at 45cm (18in). The fast-growing brassica roots soon colonize the space and from late summer, leaf growth is significant. You can also opt for Savoy cabbage or Brussels sprouts; the latter need 60cm (24in) between plants. You can sow spring onions and kale from mid-spring to early summer, although later sowings of spring onions can suffer mildew on the leaves. They are ready 5–8 weeks after transplanting, after which the kale harvests from late summer through autumn and winter. For 5–6 weeks after transplanting I cover the area with garden mesh of the closest weave to keep out flea beetles and aphids, as well as cabbage white butterflies.

GROWING TIP

Harvest the outer leaves from the bottom of the kale plants as soon as they develop fully. This keeps plants cropping for the longest period.

CULTIVARS

SPRING ONION See p.53.

KALE

'Dazzling Blue' A cavolo nero type kale with upright, blue-green stalks bearing lush and tender leaves.

'Nero di Toscana' Cavolo nero type with lance-shaped, dark grey-green blistered leaves, forming an impressive plant for months.

'Red Russian' Flatter leaves that have a purple hue, especially tender picked small, when they are ideal for eating raw in salads.

KEY INFORMATION

SPRING ONION See p.53.

KALE

Seed to harvest: 10–12 weeks **Seed to transplanting:** 3–4 weeks **Position:** Sun but tolerates some shade **Spacing:** 45cm (18in) **Hardiness:** Very hardy

Salad onions and Brussels sprouts, two weeks after they were transplanted.

TIMINGS

SPRING ONION

Sowing: Mid-May to June (under cover)
Transplanting: Early June to mid-July
Harvesting: Early July to late August

KALE

Sowing: Early May to early June (under cover)
Transplanting: Late May to early June to mid-July **Harvesting:** Mid-July to November, and possibly to March, depending on winter weather and the type of kale

ROCKET *between* LEAF LETTUCE

COMPANION TYPE: OVERLAP (4–8 weeks)

This combination is a good choice for small spaces. Salad rocket is transplanted between lettuce being harvested for their outer leaves. The rocket can be harvested from September, often while you are cropping the final leaves from lettuce sown in early June, into October.

Harvesting lettuce for its outer leaves provides space to transplant salad rocket in August, or to sow direct. I favour rocket transplanted at two weeks old, multi-sown with 3 seeds per cell. Direct sowing increases the risk of flea beetle damage, while there are few flea beetles on under cover sowings, resulting in healthy, strong seedlings. I like to pick outer leaves of rocket as you get a longer harvest than thickly sown, cut-and-come-again plants. Lettuce plants need twisting out at some point in September, depending on selection, at the time you start picking rocket.

ALTERNATIVE CHOICES

Swap salad rocket for mustards, land cress, and herbs such as dill and coriander (see p.110). Salad rocket will also grow well between ridge cucumber and fennel (see p.86).

CULTIVARS

SALAD ROCKET

Most seeds of salad rocket (*Eruca sativa*) are sold without a cultivar name. Don't use wild rocket (*Diplotaxis tenuifolia*), which grows and harvests too late for this combination.

'Apollo' Flat, rounded leaves that are not too serrated and have a good peppery flavour.

LETTUCE See p.115.

KEY INFORMATION

SALAD ROCKET

Seed to harvest: 4 weeks **Seed to transplanting:** 2 weeks **Position:** sun or part shade **Spacing:** 22cm (8½in) for multi-sown transplants, or sow in rows between lettuce and thin to 5–10cm (2–4in) between plants **Hardiness:** Hardy, will stand moderate frost

LETTUCE

Seed to harvest: 6 weeks **Seed to transplanting:** 3–4 weeks **Position:** Sun or part shade **Spacing:** Rows 22cm (8½in) **Hardiness:** Hardy but won't stand regular frost

TIMINGS

SALAD ROCKET

Sowing: Early to mid-August, direct or multi-sown in modules under cover
Transplanting: Mid- to late August
Harvesting: September to November

LETTUCE

Sowing: Late May to early June (under cover)
Transplanting: Mid-June to early July
Harvesting: Mid-July to September

WINTER SQUASH *with* AUTUMN RASPBERRY

COMPANION TYPE: BONUS

Sometimes nature gives hints for successful planting combinations. One summer I allowed trailing stems of winter squash 'Crown Prince' to grow through my productive nine-year-old autumn raspberry bed, with great results I had not expected.

Autumn raspberries don't grow much in early summer and I find them easier to keep upright if the canes are not too tall, so don't worry to water them in a dry spring. I grow the crops in adjacent beds separated by a 40cm (16in) path, and the squash stems trail across the ground and over the raspberries, reducing their size. These are autumn raspberries (as opposed to summer-cropping selections) that are cut to ground level in winter and don't need tying in. In June, the squash can appear to be covering the raspberries too much. In July, I begin to water the raspberries, their stems growing above the squash leaves. From late July until autumn we enjoy a fantastic raspberry harvest, while big grey squashes ripen underneath and around them. Winter squash can also be combined with taller soft fruits, such as currants.

CULTIVARS

WINTER SQUASH See p.63.

RASPBERRY

These are autumn-fruiting selections of *Rubus idaeus*.

'All Gold' Attractive, sweet-flavoured yellow fruit.

'Autumn Bliss' Classic selection, giving delicious large berries.

'Joan J' Spine-free canes bearing heavy crops of sweet fruit over a long period.

KEY INFORMATION

WINTER SQUASH See p.63.

RASPBERRY

Planting to harvest: Perennial **Position:** Tolerates full sun, best in dappled shade **Spacing:** 60cm (24in) **Hardiness:** Hardy

TIMINGS

WINTER SQUASH

Sowing: Mid-April (under cover) **Transplanting:** First half of May (best planted under fleece) **Harvesting:** September to October

RASPBERRY

Planting: Through winter, or March, which I favour **Harvesting:** Late July to mid-October

GROWING TIP

Raspberries are invasive. Install metal bed edging or similar around your raspberry patch, sunk to around 15cm (6in) deep to keep roots in the bed. I do not grow autumn raspberries below netting as the birds are more interested now by blackberries and elderberries in nearby hedges.

Overleaf: Early September after a very dry spring and summer, but 8cm (3in) rain in the last 12 days enabled amazing growth, also thanks to no dig.

DILL *between* ENDIVE

COMPANION TYPE: INTERPLANTING

This attractive interplanting combination balances the tall and graceful growth of dill with the low-growing, ruffled foliage of endive, an excellent autumn salad crop. Both plants can be cropped for many weeks well into late autumn.

I find dill a most pleasing autumn herb, its feathery aniseed-scented leaves casting only light shade on plants below. This combination was born out of necessity, because I had nowhere else to transplant dill that I had sown in August. Endive is often grown to produce a big heart or head, with slightly blanched leaves, and cut off cleanly at ground level. However, by picking individual leaves as you might lettuce, plants crop for longer. From an early July sowing we start picking outer leaves from August. There is enough space and growth potential for the dill transplants to thrive, harvesting for most of autumn while still cropping endive. You could easily substitute dill for coriander, and/or July-sown parsley. Parsley is winter hardy in temperate climates, so good value for spring picking.

GROWING TIP

In summer, sowing and growing plants such as dill under cover and transplanting them out into vegetable beds is often more reliable than direct sowing. I find you have more control over growth conditions for the seedlings, and use less water because they are in a small space together.

CULTIVARS

DILL

There are a few named varieties of dill (*Anethum graveolens*) but I've noticed little significant difference between them. Any will do.

ENDIVE

'Bubikopf' and **'Diva'** Escarole varieties with soft green leaves.

'Pancalieri' Frisée variety with lush, deeply indented leaves.

'Wallone' Long-cropping, frisée variety with dark green leaves.

KEY INFORMATION

DILL

Seed to harvest: 6 weeks (13 for whole heads)
Seed to transplanting: 3 weeks **Position:** Sun
Spacing: 25cm (10in) **Hardiness:** Half hardy

ENDIVE

Seed to harvest: 6–8 weeks **Seed to transplanting:** 3 weeks **Position:** Sun
Spacing: 25cm (10in) **Hardiness:** Hardy but frost may damage leaf margins

TIMINGS

DILL

Sowing: Mid- to late August for transplants, or direct sow at that time
Transplanting: Early to mid-September
Harvesting: Late September to November

ENDIVE

Sowing: 10 July to early August for transplants **Transplanting:** August
Harvesting: September to November

ENDIVE *near* LEAF LETTUCE

COMPANION TYPE: OVERLAP (3–5 weeks)

For salad over a long period, later-cropping endive is able to establish while you are still harvesting the last lettuce leaves. The endive can be planted in the gaps between lettuce plants at the same spacing.

Here is a combination that contradicts the belief that new plantings should be of a different plant family to reduce risks of pests and disease, and to balance nutrient uptake. Endive and lettuce are closely related, and I have found new endive can be planted between lettuce plants that are regularly harvested for their outer leaves. Aim to plant the endive about a month before you expect the lettuce harvests to finish. I pick my endive in the same way as lettuce, and for a week or two in late September I can be harvesting both at the same time, making it a great pairing for a small vegetable bed. Alternatively swap endive for 'Castelfranco' chicory, for winter harvest, or spinach (see p.104).

GROWING TIP

As an alternative to harvesting the outer leaves of endive, you can also leave them to make a heart. They are at their best during late autumn and make delicious salads, the inner heart leaves being slightly blanched and less bitter.

Endive establishing in September between lettuce, which have given ten weeks of harvests already.

CULTIVARS

ENDIVE See p.125.

LETTUCE See p.115.

KEY INFORMATION

ENDIVE See p.125.

LETTUCE

Seed to harvest: 6 weeks **Seed to transplanting:** 3–4 weeks **Position:** Full sun or light shade **Spacing:** 22–25cm (8½–10in) **Hardiness:** Hardy but won't stand regular frost

TIMINGS

ENDIVE

Sowing: Late July to early August (under cover) **Transplanting:** Mid- to late August **Harvesting:** September to November

LETTUCE

Sowing: Late May to early June (under cover) **Transplanting:** Mid-June to early July **Harvesting:** July to late September

BROAD BEAN *beside* ASPARAGUS

COMPANION TYPE: BONUS, COVER CROP

Cover crops and green manures are planted to improve soil, boosting levels of carbon while providing other benefits such as suppressing weed growth. Growing broad beans beside established asparagus adds nitrogen from their root nodules into the soil, in addition to carbon, benefiting the asparagus.

Asparagus is tall and slender, but I find it is a thirsty crop after midsummer. Before that, you can crop fast-maturing spears (see p.58). Pop broad bean seed into 5cm (2in) deep dibbed holes in early autumn, along either side of the asparagus. You may need to water in order to encourage germination and early growth. In October, asparagus loses its foliage and beans that have their roots in the soil grow quickly; by November you will have quite tall plants. They are too big to survive winter and will be killed by frost, slowly rotting back into ground. It's a quick and easy method. White mustard (*Sinapis alba*) is another easy green manure (see p.136); scatter seed around and through asparagus before early October.

GROWING TIP

Broad beans are slow to start growing and seeds need to be in the ground before the middle of September for worthwhile growth before winter. If plants survive winter, you can crop beans in May, but they can smother some new asparagus as it comes through the soil surface.

CULTIVARS

Any asparagus and any broad bean. This is a useful way of using up saved broad bean seed, or surplus seed of the current year. Rather than throwing seed away you will be putting it to good use, improving the soil.

KEY INFORMATION

BROAD BEAN

Seed to harvest: The beans are not grown for harvest; duration in growth depends on frost **Position:** Will stand some shade **Spacing:** Direct sow seeds 10–15cm (4–6in) apart, 30cm (12in) from the asparagus **Hardiness:** Hardy, but damaged by moderate frost

ASPARAGUS See p.59.

TIMINGS

BROAD BEAN

Sowing: September; early is best

ASPARAGUS

Sowing: February to March (under cover) **Transplanting:** June to July. Alternatively, plant crowns March to April, which may bring harvesting forward by a year **Harvesting:** End of April, May, and June, until the summer solstice

By early November, we have cut down the old asparagus stems and the broad beans are still growing.

ALTERNATIVE CHOICE

Spinach sown in August, and transplanted up to mid-September, can survive winter and crop in spring.

CHERVIL *with* BROAD BEAN

COMPANION TYPE: OVERLAP (up to 16 weeks if chervil overwinters)

With its soft, fern-like, aniseed-flavoured bright green foliage, chervil is a useful and easily raised herb best grown in the cooler conditions of autumn. It overlaps well with direct-sown broad beans that overwinter to provide early spring harvests.

Chervil is a fantastic herb; when sown in late summer, I find it overwinters and continues to crop in early spring. It can be slow to start, so if direct sowing I'd suggest growing in rows in order to see the tiny seedlings and weed around them. I prefer to raise plants under cover as transplants and set out at 22cm (8½in). Direct sow (or transplant if you prefer) broad beans between the chervil in late autumn. You'll find the beans are also slow at first but this allows time for your chervil harvest; the aim is simply to overwinter small broad bean plants for spring cropping. Sowing broad beans in late autumn provides early crops and reduces damage from blackfly and rust. Cut down chervil by early April as plants go to seed in spring.

CULTIVARS

CHERVIL

Seldom sold with cultivar names, but look out for curled and plain (flat-leaved) types. They have similar growth habits and flavour.

BROAD BEAN

Choose a reliably winter hardy cultivar if planting out in autumn. My favourite is 'Aquadulce Claudia', and there are several others possible.

KEY INFORMATION

CHERVIL

Seed to harvest: 7–8 weeks **Seed to transplanting:** 4 weeks **Position:** Sun or part shade **Spacing:** 22cm (8½in) **Hardiness:** Hardy to −10°C (14°F)

BROAD BEAN

Seed to harvest: 24–26 weeks **Position:** Sun or part shade **Spacing:** 30cm (12in) **Hardiness:** Hardy but freezing weather can damage plants

In late November, chervil is still strong and broad beans are establishing before winter.

TIMINGS

CHERVIL

Sowing: August (direct or under cover as a transplant) **Transplanting:** September **Harvesting:** Late September to October, and until early April if plants survive winter

BROAD BEAN

Direct sowing: Late October to early November (I aim for 28 October– 5 November) **Harvesting:** June, even by late May if spring is warm

CORIANDER *between* AUTUMN LETTUCE

COMPANION TYPE: OVERLAP (7 weeks if coriander raised from seed, 5 weeks from transplants)

I find coriander surprisingly hardy, cropping outside through winter and into early spring, especially if it can be protected. This makes it suitable for overlap planting with any salads that will finish before winter, such as lettuce.

Coriander is often used as an autumn salad plant, but it can easily crop for longer as it thrives in temperate winters. Planting with lettuce harvested for outer leaves works well as it maintains space for the coriander transplants. The coriander will not grow big while lettuce is taking most of the nutrients, but during October lettuce begins to fade; I aim to twist out remaining plants and remove weeds by 20 October, which leaves a bed of coriander almost ready for its initial harvest.

CULTIVARS

CORIANDER See p.37.

LETTUCE
Any cultivar of lettuce can be used, but I recommend Batavian types as they resist mildew in autumn.

KEY INFORMATION

CORIANDER See p.37.
LETTUCE See p.75.

TIMINGS

CORIANDER
Sowing: Mid-August (under cover)
Transplanting: Early September
Harvesting: Late October to April (if plants survive winter)

LETTUCE
Sowing: Mid-July, ideally 15–20 July (under cover) **Transplanting:** Early August
Harvesting: Early September to 20 October

GARLIC *between* WINTER SALAD

COMPANION TYPE: INTERPLANTING

The timing of interplanting garlic with winter salads under cover ties in nicely with summer crops such as tomatoes and cucumbers both finishing in early October, and being planted again in May. This combination feels like a free harvest, because all the plant spacings would be exactly the same without the garlic. And it's so easy.

Winter salads include a range of crops (see p.134) and when grown under cover in a greenhouse or polytunnel, as in this example, plants provide regular harvests through winter. The garlic goes in the ground by the middle of October, just after the salads are transplanted. I don't allow any extra space for it, dropping cloves into dibbed holes in a line up the centre of 1.2m (4ft) wide middle beds in a polytunnel, and the 1.5m (5ft) wide middle bed in my greenhouse. The only maintenance of garlic plants through winter and early spring is to remove occasional yellowing leaves that fall on the salad plants. These are usually large enough by late November to be picked of a few outer leaves, or cut in the case of *Claytonia*. In December we often take two harvests, the last one around the winter solstice, and then through January plants are more dormant, depending on temperature. If it's really cold, we lay fleece directly on top. Harvests continue every second week through February, and then weekly in March until the second half of April.

ALTERNATIVE CHOICES

Instead of garlic, try multi-sown spring onions sown early to mid-September, or onion sets for autumn planting.

After the salad is removed

By April the garlic is quite large and from the middle of the month the salad starts rising to flower, so we twist out plants. Now the garlic has more space, making significant growth. In early to mid-May, we transplant tomatoes and cucumbers in lines, on either side of the garlic line, and they coexist for about a month. Softneck garlic is ready by early June, when the bulbs are often very large. Partly that's from the extra shelter and warmth, partly it's because garlic under cover does not suffer rust so much as garlic outdoors.

CULTIVARS

GARLIC See p.82.

WINTER SALAD

I grow various different crops under cover for winter salad leaves. I recommend lettuce (cultivars such as 'Red Grenoble', 'Winter Density', 'Marvel of Four Seasons', 'Nevada', and 'Charles'), endive (cultivars such as 'Diva', 'Pancalieri', and 'Wallone'), spinach ('Medania'), mustards, salad rocket, land cress, winter purslane (*Claytonia*), chard, spinach, coriander, and chervil.

TIMINGS

GARLIC

Planting: (From cloves) mid-October
Harvesting: Early June (softneck), late June (hardneck); timings vary with cultivar

WINTER SALAD

Sowing: 10–20 September **Transplanting:** Mid-October **Harvesting:** November to late April

KEY INFORMATION

GARLIC See p.82.

WINTER SALAD

Seed to harvest: 8–10 weeks **Seed to transplanting:** 4 weeks **Position:** Sunny unheated greenhouse or polytunnel **Spacing:** 22cm (8½in) **Hardiness:** Stands light frost

April in the polytunnel: lettuce and endive with garlic growing between, all planted in October.

WHITE MUSTARD *with* GARLIC

COMPANION TYPE: COVER CROP

The beauty of white mustard as a cover crop or green manure is that it is conveniently killed by temperatures of around −5°C (23°F). While the garlic establishes slowly, the mustard germinates and grows quickly, then is killed off by the first hard frosts of winter, leaving the bed clear for the garlic.

White mustard (*Sinapis alba*) is a free harvest of carbon for the soil. After it dies, the mustard decomposes on the surface, leaving a residue of straw-like stems while the roots decay in soil, adding organic matter. While not a nitrogen-fixing choice, white mustard is easier to manage than other cover crops that need mulching or removing in spring, when many prove hard to get rid of. If a few mustard plants survive, they are easily pulled out by hand.

Sow the mustard and plant your garlic before mid-October to allow at least six weeks of growing time before conditions get too dark and cold. You will get 40–60cm (16–24in) high mustard plants. I like to plant my garlic, spread compost on top to ensure fertility for a year of cropping, then scatter mustard seed on top. Garlic offers many succession choices and you may decide to plant celeriac or beetroot between it the following spring.

CULTIVARS

WHITE MUSTARD

For garden use as a cover crop, seed is simply sold as white mustard.

GARLIC See p.82.

KEY INFORMATION

WHITE MUSTARD

Seed to harvest: No harvest, grows until frost **Position:** Sun or part shade **Spacing:** Sow seeds 3–5cm (1¼–2in) apart **Hardiness:** Hardy to around −4°C (25°F).

GARLIC See p.82.

TIMINGS

WHITE MUSTARD

Direct sowing: Spring to autumn, but to grow with garlic, direct sow late September to mid-October

GARLIC

Sowing: Early to mid-October (November would be too late for this combination)
Harvesting: 10–20 June (softneck), early July (hardneck); timings vary with cultivar, climate, and incidence of rust disease

---

GROWING TIP

Once the mustard has germinated, check the bed carefully for weeds such as bitter cress, chickweed, and groundsel. They are best removed before they get too big, a quick job because their roots pull out easily from soft compost. Once the mustard has grown up it will suppress most weeds.

GARLIC *between* LEAF LETTUCE

COMPANION TYPE: OVERLAP (2–4 weeks)

Versatile garlic will establish in autumn with little light initially, which makes it suitable for popping in between other crops that are close to finishing, in this case lettuce. This is an easy and useful overlap for late in the year, and will work well in small plots.

In autumn you can plant garlic cloves from late September until November. During the early part of this period, late summer plantings of lettuce, picked for outer leaves, are coming towards their finish point. Use a dibber to make 3cm (1¼in) holes between the lettuce and drop garlic cloves in, push them down, and cover. Because the garlic is spaced more closely than salad plants, at around 15cm (6in) apart, I plant on the diagonal line between salad plants on a square spacing. Rows across a bed do not work, because you keep bumping into salad plants. You can also grow in lines along a bed, although it's harder to reach the middle row.

ALTERNATIVE CHOICES

Swap the garlic for endive (see p.126), salad rocket, or *Claytonia*, and scatter seed of white mustard (*Sinapis alba*) between the lettuce for a green manure cover (see p.136).

CULTIVARS

GARLIC See p.82.

LETTUCE See p.75.

KEY INFORMATION

GARLIC See p.82.

LATE SUMMER TO AUTUMN LETTUCE

Seed to harvest: 6 weeks **Seed to transplanting:** 3–4 weeks **Position:** Sun or light shade **Spacing:** 23–25cm (9–10in) **Hardiness:** Hardy but won't stand regular frost

TIMINGS

GARLIC

Planting: (From cloves) early October

Harvesting: 10–20 June (softneck), early July (hardneck); timings vary with cultivar, climate, and incidence of rust disease

LATE SUMMER TO AUTUMN LETTUCE

Sowing: Mid-July **Transplanting:** Early August **Harvesting:** Late August to October

The spacing of new garlic, before planting between lettuce, which will finish cropping soon.

AUTUMN SALAD *with* ONIONS *or* SPRING ONION

COMPANION TYPE: OVERLAP (2–4 weeks for bulb onions, 6–8 weeks for spring onions), INTERPLANTING

There are two options here. Either overlap salads for autumn between maincrop bulb onions, which finish from mid- to late summer, or interplant spring onions with July-planted autumn salads. The onions finish before salad plants need all the space.

For autumn salads I recommend cultivars of chicory, which can produce nicely blanched radicchio, in open ground and without the extra work of forcing. They can be planted in early to mid-July and that timing works with onions finishing soon after. They grow tight heads of beautiful colour, which store for up to six weeks after harvest. Another option is to transplant multi-sown salad onions for harvest in early autumn, between autumn salads, which continue growing. Sow the onions at summer solstice. All of these grow easily, and use space efficiently.

GROWING TIPS

Use the chicory cultivars listed and sow no earlier than 8 June, to minimize bolting in early autumn. In autumn, salad onions can be prone to mildew on leaves. Cultivars of *Allium cepa*, such as 'White Lisbon', stay healthier than *Allium fistulosum* types such as 'Ishikura' (see p.53).

CULTIVARS

CHICORY/RADICCHIO

'Castelfranco' More open, very pretty, and stands frost well until March.

'506TT' Firm, bright red heads from October.

'206TT' Long, pointed, dark red Treviso-type heads from October.

ONION/SPRING ONION

'Apache' Crisp salad onion with deep purple-red skins and a mild flavour.

'Red Baron' Bulb onion with a deep red colour, either from seed or sets. Stores well.

'White Lisbon' Salad onion with long white stems to harvest small at this time of year.

KEY INFORMATION

CHICORY/RADICCHIO

Seed to harvest: 13–16 weeks **Seed to transplanting:** 3 weeks **Position:** Sun or part shade **Spacing:** 30cm (12in) **Hardiness:** Hardy to −3°C (27°F)

ONIONS/SPRING ONION

Seed to harvest: 20–24 weeks (9–11 weeks for spring onions) **Seed to transplanting:** 5–6 weeks **Position:** Sun or part shade **Spacing:** 25–30cm (10–12in) between multi-sown clumps; plant sets in rows across the bed, 10–15cm (4–6in) between onions, rows 30cm (12in) apart **Hardiness:** Hardy

TIMINGS

CHICORY/RADICCHIO

Sowing: 8 June to 5 July
Transplanting: Late June to late July
Harvesting: Mid-September to November, and to March for 'Castelfranco'

ONIONS/SPRING ONION

Sowing: Ideally 20 February to early March (sow spring onions mid-June)
Transplanting: End March to early April (plant out spring onions mid-July)
Harvesting: Mid-July to early August (pull spring onions end of August)

CLAYTONIA *and* CORN SALAD *between* SWEDE

COMPANION TYPE: INTERPLANTING

Swedes survive in the ground through winter, for harvest as late as March. During this time there is space between them for interplanting winter salads. *Claytonia* (or winter purslane) and corn salad (lamb's lettuce) are ideal, as you can sow or transplant them in mid-September, having first removed some lower leaves from the swedes.

Claytonia and corn salad grow tender, mild-tasting leaves, which are so welcome for eating raw in winter, when fresh greens are scarce. Each plant produces many small leaves on long stems (*Claytonia*) or short (corn salad). Harvest them taking care to leave baby leaves below the cut level, to enable regrowth. Pop in seeds or transplants between maturing swede plants in autumn. In winter, you might have three or four worthwhile harvests from each salad plant. After any period of sustained frosts (below about −4°C/25°F) some *Claytonia* leaves will discolour, but you can reduce this by covering plants with fleece. All these survive frost. Chervil, coriander, or salad onions could all be substituted for the *Claytonia*.

GROWING TIP

As autumn advances, twist off lower foliage from the swedes, which is starting to decay, to free space for sowing or transplanting the *Claytonia*.

CULTIVARS

CLAYTONIA
Seed is simply sold as *Claytonia perfoliata*.

CORN SALAD See p.151.

SWEDE
'Marian' and **'Gowrie'** Old, open-pollinated cultivars that grow consistently fine roots.

'Tweed' F1 Some resistance to club root.

Late November: corn salad sown in early September between swedes.

KEY INFORMATION

CLAYTONIA

Seed to harvest: 70 days **Seed to transplanting:** 4–5 weeks **Position:** Sun or part shade **Spacing:** 15cm (6in) **Hardiness:** Hardy to −8°C (18°F) with no snow cover

CORN SALAD See p.151.

SWEDE

Seed to harvest: 150 days **Seed to transplanting:** 3–4 weeks **Position:** Sun or part shade **Spacing:** 30cm (12in) **Hardiness:** Hardy to −10°C (14°F), colder with snow cover

TIMINGS

CLAYTONIA

Sowing: September **Transplanting:** October **Harvesting:** Mid-November to April

CORN SALAD See p.151.

SWEDE

Sowing: May to mid-June **Transplanting:** Late May to June **Harvesting:** November to March

WINTER SALAD *and* VEG *between* TOMATO

COMPANION TYPE: OVERLAP (2–4 weeks)

This overlap combination for use under cover allows you to get winter crops growing in the space between tomato plants that are still cropping. This increases growing and establishment time, as the days shorten and cool rapidly.

Every autumn in the polytunnel, I transplant winter salads such as lettuce, endive, and salad rocket, as well as leaf vegetables including chard and spinach, to crop regularly until April. It's important for them to grow strong roots before conditions turn colder and darker in November. If there is any delay in planting, subsequent growth of these winter crops is much reduced. By popping them in spaces between by now leafless lower stems of tomato plants you can get a head start. When they have finished, before the frosts return, be careful when removing the tomato stems, cutting around and under the main roots close to the surface as you lift them out, for minimal disturbance of your establishing winter crops.

CULTIVARS

WINTER SALAD

I recommend chervil, coriander, endive (see p.125), land cress, lettuce (such as 'Red Grenoble', 'Winter Density', 'Marvel of Four Seasons', 'Red Velvet'), mustards both red and green, salad rocket, spinach (grown for smaller leaves), and winter purslane (*Claytonia*).

WINTER LEAF VEGETABLES

The following can be grown under cover at this time: chard, kale, spring onions, spinach.

TOMATO See p.39.

KEY INFORMATION

WINTER SALAD

Seed to harvest: 8–10 weeks **Seed to transplanting:** 4 weeks **Position:** Sunny greenhouse or polytunnel **Spacing:** 22cm (8½in) **Hardiness:** Stands light frost

WINTER LEAF VEGETABLES

Seed to harvest: 9–10 weeks **Seed to transplanting:** 4 weeks **Position:** Sunny greenhouse or polytunnel **Spacing:** 30cm (12in) **Hardiness:** Stands light frost

TOMATO

Seed to harvest: 15–17 weeks **Seed to transplanting:** 6–8 weeks **Position:** Sunny greenhouse or polytunnel **Spacing:** 45–50cm (18–20in) **Hardiness:** Frost tender

TIMINGS

WINTER SALAD

Sowing: Early to mid-September (under cover) **Transplanting:** Early to mid-October **Harvesting:** November to late April

WINTER LEAF VEGETABLES

Sowing: Mid-August (under cover)
Transplanting: Mid-September
Harvesting: Mid-October to late April

TOMATO

Sowing: Mid-March (under cover)
Transplanting: Early May **Harvesting:** July to mid-October

KALE *between* ONION

COMPANION TYPE: OVERLAP (4 weeks, depending on onion cultivar)

As with garlic, maincrop bulb onions are predictable in maturing times, and they allow plenty of light through for this overlap planting. Kale sown in May works nicely as a transplant between bulb onions, which mature around four weeks after the kale. Timings of onion harvest depend on the cultivar, and whether you use sets or seeds to grow them.

Onions and garlic serve really well as larger, host plants because light penetrates between their leaves, helping new plants to establish. On the downside, this also allows weeds to grow, but this is where no dig really scores, as weeds are easier to remove. Act as soon as weeds are seen. I find onions multi-sown around 20 February are ready to transplant within a month, and I lay fleece over to help them establish. Over several years of using this companion planting my kale have grown fine without covers, with only some flea beetle damage when plants are small.

GROWING TIP

When you see a few onion tops falling over and lying on the ground, it's a sign to push the others over to help dry their necks. About a week later, gently twist them to detach their roots. Leave them on the ground for another week to dry further, or move to a ventilated place under cover. Either way, your kale now has full light.

Late June: multi-sown onions with kale recently planted between.

CULTIVARS

ONION See p.79.

KALE

'Cavolo Nero' Beautiful deep green, blistered foliage, and pale stalks. There can be variation between seed packets; some plants grow tall with long, thin, drooping leaves, while those with a compact habit and fleshy leaves are more productive.

'Dwarf Green Curled' Compact selection perfect for smaller gardens.

'Red Russian' Classic kale with purple-tinged leaves that are tender at all stages, but especially when picked small to eat raw.

KEY INFORMATION

ONION See p.79.

KALE See p.117.

TIMINGS

ONION

Sowing: Ideally 20 February to early March (under cover) **Transplanting:** End March to early April **Harvesting:** Mid-July to early August (depending on cultivar)

KALE

Sowing: Early to mid-May
Transplanting: Mid-June
Harvesting: August to March

ALTERNATIVES

Other brassicas, such as cabbage for autumn or Brussels sprouts. Try beetroot or direct-sown carrots at the same time the onions are transplanted.

Harvesting onions in July. You can also see mature carrots, and kale which I had transplanted in mid-June.

CORN SALAD *under* CABBAGE

COMPANION TYPE: OVERLAP (4–8 weeks)

The autumn season has fewer options for companion planting, with not many seeds starting. This one has worked well for me over several years: corn salad (lamb's lettuce) sown or transplanted between and underneath cabbage or other brassicas such as autumn broccoli or swede. Corn salad is incredibly hardy, so the harvest season is long and worthwhile.

Either draw lines 2cm (¾in) deep in the surface, to drop corn salad seeds into spaced at 1 seed per 2cm (¾in), with rows 20cm (8in) apart, or raise transplants to pop in at an equidistant 5–7cm (2–2¾in). Direct sowing is easier and quicker, and it's usually damp enough in early autumn for seeds to germinate well, even from simply scattering them on the surface around brassica plants, with a light raking, or a little new compost on top. Seedlings grow strongly in early autumn. The last sowing date for the corn salad is mid-September and by mid- to late autumn some will be ready to cut. Salad harvests continue all winter, say from late November to early April. We cut plants here and there from the bed, to thin them out and allow neighbouring plants to grow larger for subsequent cuts.

GROWING TIP

To remove cabbage after a harvest of the head, I use a spade to chop through the thick roots, no more than 7cm (2¾in) from the stem. Or you can twist carefully to snap off the main roots and remove the stem without much disturbance of the corn salad. Small roots stay in the soil to feed the corn salad.

CULTIVARS

CORN SALAD

Buy packet seed or collect your own seed in late May of any cultivar after leaving 10 or more plants to flower in late April – worthwhile for plants adapted to your winter conditions.

'D'Olanda' Larger, rather less dense leaves than usual.

'Verte de Cambrai' and **'Vit'** Widely available and reliable cultivars.

CABBAGE

Choose cabbage cultivars listed as suitable for autumn cropping, rather than winter Savoys, which leave less space for the corn salad.

'Filderkraut' White autumn cabbage sown in May. Large pointed heads of sweet leaves.

'Golden Acre' Medium heads for late autumn, from sowing in midsummer.

'Red Rodynda' Red cabbage forming compact plants with firm heads for late autumn harvests.

KEY INFORMATION

CORN SALAD

Seed to harvest: 80+ days **Seed to transplanting:** 35 days **Position:** Sun or part shade **Spacing:** 5–7cm (2–2¾in) **Hardiness:** Frost hardy

CABBAGE

Seed to harvest: 160–180 days **Seed to transplanting:** 3–4 weeks **Position:** Sun or part shade **Spacing:** 45cm (18in) or 35cm (14in) for 'Golden Acre' **Hardiness:** Frost hardy

TIMINGS

CORN SALAD

Sowing: Early to mid-September
Transplanting: Late September to mid-October **Harvesting:** November to mid-April

CABBAGE

Sowing: Early May, or early July for 'Golden Acre' **Transplanting:** June
Harvesting: October to November

Overleaf: Sunflowers continue to thrive in early autumn, while cool-weather vegetables, such as kale, start to give good harvests, and winter squash is soon ready to pick.

INDEX

A
Allium leaf miner 43
aphids 43
asparagus
 asparagus interplanted with turnips 58–59
 broad beans beside asparagus 128–29
autumn 124–51
autumn lettuce, coriander between 132
autumn salad with onions or spring onions 78, 140–41

B
bacteria 14, 17
beetroot 21, 101, 148
 beetroot between garlic 82–83
 beetroot between onions 78–79, 84
 broccoli with interplanted beetroot 80–81
 melons between beetroot 56–57
 multi-sowing 13, 14, 30
 ridge cucumber between potatoes and beetroot 92–93
 spring onions between beetroot 52–55
 succession planting 13, 31
birds 24, 121
bitter cress 137
brassicas 26
 sowing seeds 22
 transplanting 24
 see also individual types of brassicas
broad beans 21, 31, 90
 broad beans beside asparagus 128–29
 chervil with broad beans 130–31
broccoli with interplanted beetroot 80–81
Brussels sprouts 148
 Brussels sprouts between carrots 32–35

C
cabbage 21, 148
 corn salad under cabbage 150–51
 Savoy cabbage between onions 84–85
cabbage root fly 60, 65, 76
calabrese 21
Calendula officinalis 68
carbon 12, 16, 128, 136
carrot root fly 33
carrots 58, 90, 148
 Brussels sprouts between carrots 32–35
 carrots between lettuce 72–75, 101
 direct sowing 20
 radishes intersown with carrots 31, 76–77
 succession planting 31
catch crops 13
caterpillars 26
celeriac
 celeriac between garlic 40–41
 celeriac between lettuce 46–47
 leeks between celeriac 42–45
 spring onions between celeriac 42, 52
celery
 celery between lettuce 114–15
 Chinese pink celery 115
Centaurea cyanus 68
chard 134, 145
 chard between dwarf French beans 96–99
chervil 134, 142, 145
 chervil with broad beans 130–31
chickweed 137
chicory 22, 78, 140
Claytonia (winter purslane) 134, 138, 145
 Claytonia and corn salad between swede 142–43
coir 21
cold tolerant vegetables 21
companion plantings 13
compost 16, 108
 mixing your own blend 21
 potting mixes 21
 worm compost 21
coriander 84, 118, 134, 142, 145
 coriander between autumn lettuce 132
 coriander between garlic 36–37
 dill and coriander under cordon cucumbers 110–13
corn salad
 Claytonia and corn salad between swede 142–43
 corn salad under cabbage 150–51
cornflowers 68
cotyledons 22
courgettes 21, 26, 31, 90
 courgettes between turnips 64
cover crops 12, 128
crop rotation 16–17
cucumbers 21

dill and coriander under
    cordon cucumbers
    110–13
fennel between ridge
    cucumbers 86–89
ridge cucumbers between
    potatoes and beetroot
    92–93
ridge cucumbers between
    strawberries and peas
    90–91

D
Dianthus 68
digging 16, 17
dill 118
    dill between endives
        124–25
    dill and coriander under
        cordon cucumbers
        110–13
direct sowing 13, 20, 26
diseases 26
    rust 83
    Septoria disease 40, 43
dwarf French beans
    chard between dwarf
        French beans 96–99
    dwarf French beans
        between fennel 94–95
    dwarf French beans
        between lettuce 100–101
dwarf French marigolds
    68–69

E
endives 78, 138, 144, 145
    dill between endives
        124–25
    endives near leaf lettuce
        126–27

F
fennel 58
    dwarf French beans
        between fennel 94–95
    fennel between ridge

cucumbers 86–89
fennel between spinach
    48–49
flea beetles 26, 76, 80, 118, 147
fleece 24, 25, 60, 62, 65, 76, 92
Florence fennel 58
    dwarf French beans
        between fennel 94–95
    fennel between ridge
        cucumbers 86–89
    fennel between spinach
        48–49
French beans 21
    chard between dwarf
        French beans 96–99
    dwarf French beans
        between fennel 94–95
    dwarf French beans
        between lettuce 100–101
French marigolds, dwarf
    varieties 68–69
frost
    frost tolerant vegetables 21
    last frost dates 25
fungi 17

G
garlic
    beetroot between garlic
        82–83
    celeriac between garlic
        40–41
    cordon tomatoes between
        garlic 38–39
    coriander between garlic
        36–37
    garlic between leaf lettuce
        138–39
    garlic between winter salad
        133–35
    white mustard with garlic
        136–37
germination 20
green manure 128, 136, 138
groundsel 137
growing on 20

growing together
    benefits of 14
    key techniques 20–27
    methods of 12–13

H
hardening off 20
herbs 84, 118
    see individual types of herbs

I
interplanted crops 31
intersowing, succession
    planting using 13

K
kale 84, 145
    kale between onions
        147–49
    spring onions between kale
        116–17

L
land cress 118, 134, 145
leaf miner flies 43
leeks between celeriac 42–45
lettuce 21, 78, 84, 144
    carrots between lettuces
        72–75
    celeriac between lettuces
        46–47
    celery between lettuces
        114–15
    dwarf French beans
        between lettuces
        100–101
    endives near leaf lettuce
        126–27
    garlic between leaf lettuce
        138–39
    parsnips intersown between
        lettuces 109
    rocket between leaf lettuce
        118–19
    sowing seeds 22
    spinach between lettuces
        105

transplanting 24
lettuce, autumn: coriander between autumn lettuces 132

M

Malope trifida 'Vulcan' 68
manure, green 128, 136, 138
melons 21
   melons between beetroot 56–57
mesh 24, 43, 76, 80
mildew, powdery 26, 86, 110
multi-sowing 14, 30
mustard 118, 134, 138, 145
   white mustard with garlic 136–37
mycelial networks 14, 17

N

nasturtiums 68
netting 80
no dig gardening 16–17, 26, 30

O

onions 13, 14, 21, 30
   autumn salad with onions or spring onions 78, 140–41
   beetroot between onions 78–79
   kale between onions 147–49
   Savoy cabbage between onions 84–85
   transplanting 24
   see also spring onions
organic matter 16–17, 136
overlapping crops 31

P

parsley 84
parsnips 20
   parsnips intersown between lettuces 109
   parsnips intersown between spinach 106–108

peas 21, 31
   ridge cucumber between strawberries and peas 90–91
   turnips and radishes between potatoes and peas 60–61
pests 20, 24, 26
   Allium leaf miner 43
   aphids 43
   birds 24, 121
   cabbage root fly 60, 65, 76
   carrot root fly 33
   caterpillars 26
   flea beetles 26, 76, 80, 118, 147
   leaf miner flies 43
   pigeons 33
   protecting against 33
   rabbits 76
   slugs 26, 49, 72, 80
photosynthesis 12, 17, 26
pigeons 33
plant raising, phases of 20
planting out 24
pot marigolds 68
potatoes
   early spinach between potatoes 50–51
   ridge cucumbers between potatoes and beetroot 92–93
   turnips and radishes between potatoes and peas 60–61
potting mixes 21
potting on 24
powdery mildew 26, 86, 110
purple sprouting broccoli 30–31

R

rabbits 76
radicchio 140
radishes 13, 14, 30, 58

radishes intersown with carrots 76–77
transplanting 24
turnips and radishes between potatoes and peas 60–61
raspberries, winter squash with autumn 120–21
rhizophagy 17
ridge cucumbers
   fennel between ridge cucumbers 86–89
   ridge cucumbers between potatoes and beetroot 92–93
   ridge cucumbers between strawberries and peas 90–91
rocket 134, 138, 144, 145
   flea beetles 26
   rocket between leaf lettuce 118–19
runner beans 21
rust 83

S

salad, autumn: autumn salad with onions or spring onions 78, 140–41
salad, winter
   garlic between winter salad 133–35
   winter salad and veg between tomatoes 144–45
salad rocket 134, 138, 144, 145
   flea beetles 26
   rocket between leaf lettuce 118–19
Savoy cabbage between onions 84–85
seedlings, when to transplant 22
seeds
   how to sow 22, 26

multi-sowing 14, 30
  sourcing 20
Septoria disease 40, 43
Sinapis alba 136–37, 138
slugs 26, 49, 72, 80
soil
  no dig gardening 16–17, 30
  organic matter 16–17
  soil structure 17
sowing seeds 22, 26
spinach 134, 145
  early spinach between potatoes 50–51
  fennel between spinach 48–49
  parsnips intersown between spinach 106–108
  spinach between lettuce 105
  spinach under cordon tomatoes 102–104
spring 32–71
spring cabbage 31
spring onions 101, 133, 145
  autumn salad with onions or spring onions 140–41
  spring onions between beetroot 52–55
  spring onions between celeriac 42, 52
  spring onions between kale 116–17
  tomatoes between spring onions 38
squash, winter 21
  sweetcorn between winter squash 62–65
  winter squash between turnips 64–65
  winter squash with autumn raspberries 120–21
strawberries
  ridge cucumbers between strawberries and peas 90–91

succession planting 30–31
  using interplanting 13
  using intersowing 13
summer 72–123
swede, *Claytonia* and corn salad between 142–43
sweetcorn 21
  sweetcorn between winter squash 62–65

T

Tagetes patula 68–69
techniques, key 20–27
tomatoes 21, 31, 90, 101
  cordon tomatoes between garlic 38–39
  spinach under cordon tomatoes 102–104
  tomatoes between spring onions 38
  winter salad and veg between tomatoes 144–45
transplanted plants 12, 13
  how long to keep 24
  reasons for raising plants as transplants 20
  when to transplant 22
Tropaeolum majus 'Empress of India' 68
turnips 13, 14, 21, 30
  asparagus interplanted with turnips 58–59
  courgettes between turnips 64
  turnips and radishes between potatoes and peas 60–61
  winter squash between turnips 64–65

V

vegetables
  cold tolerant vegetables 21
  frost tolerant vegetables 21
  what to sow when 21

  winter salad and veg between tomatoes 144–45
  see also individual types of vegetables

W

watermelons 57
weeds and weeding 26, 137
white mustard 138
  white mustard with garlic 136–37
winter leaf vegetables
  winter salad and veg between tomatoes 144–45
winter purslane (*Claytonia*) 134, 138, 145
  Claytonia and corn salad between swede 142–43
winter salad
  garlic between winter salad 133–35
  winter salad and veg between tomatoes 144–45
winter squash
  sweetcorn between winter squash 62–65
  winter squash between turnips 64–65
  winter squash with autumn raspberries 120–21
worm compost 21

Y

yellowed leaves 22

Z

Zinnia 68

RESOURCES

BOOKS

Dowding, Charles, *Compost: Transform Waste into New Life* (Dorling Kindersley, 2024)

Dowding, Charles, *No Dig: Nurture Your Soil to Grow Better Veg with Less Effort* (Dorling Kindersley, 2022)

Gilbert, Kadeem J and Tanya Renner, *Acid or base? How do plants regulate the ecology of their phylloplane?* In *Annals of Botany Plants*, Volume 13, Issue 4, August 2021 (https://academic.oup.com/aobpla/article/13/4/plab032/6295904)

Schlanger, Zoë, *The Light Eaters: The New Science of Plant Intelligence* (HarperCollins, 2024)

Sheldrake, Merlin, *Entangled Life: How Fungi Make Our Worlds, Change Our Minds and Shape Our Futures* (Vintage, 2020)

PRODUCTS

Charles Dowding range of propagation kit from Containerwise (https://containerwise.co.uk/product-category/charles-dowding/)

Fleece and mesh covers made from plant materials by Andermatt (https://andermattgarden.co.uk), or made with plastic, from Gardening Naturally (https://gardening-naturally.com)

Copper tools in the UK, by Implementations (https://implementations.co.uk/)

Long-handled dibber from Garden Imports (https://www.gardenimports.co.uk/product/charles-dowding-long-handled-ash-dibber)

AUTHOR'S ACKNOWLEDGEMENTS

The publishing team at DK, who stimulated me to write this book in the middle of summer, which I would never have thought possible. In particular Chris Young, and Ruth O'Rourke, Alastair Laing, and Philip Clayton. Adam Wood and Anne Svenstrup who gardened so well when I was writing. Nicola Smith for key and timely help. Jason Ingram for being such fun to work with, and for capturing the beauty.

PUBLISHER'S ACKNOWLEDGEMENTS

DK would like to thank Vanessa Bird for indexing and Kathy Steer for proofreading.

PICTURE CREDITS

Dorling Kindersley: Jason Ingram: 2, 4, 7, 8, 15, 18–19, 23, 25, 27, 31, 34, 39, 44, 45, 51, 55, 65, 70–71, 74, 83, 89, 91, 93, 97, 98, 101, 112, 113, 117, 149, 152–153. All other photographs © Charles Dowding with the images on page 64 taken by Lucy Pope and page 107 by Edward Dowding.

Senior Editor Alastair Laing
Gardening Design Manager Barbara Zuniga
Production Editor Becky Fallowfield
Senior Production Controller Stephanie McConnell
Editorial Director Ruth O'Rourke
Art Director Maxine Pedliham
Publishing Director Stephanie Jackson

Editorial Clare Double
Design Geoff Borin
Consultancy Philip Clayton
Photography Jason Ingram
Woodcuts Jonathan Gibbs

First published in Great Britain in 2026 by
Dorling Kindersley Limited
20 Vauxhall Bridge Road,
London SW1V 2SA

The authorised representative in the EEA is
Dorling Kindersley Verlag GmbH. Arnulfstr. 124,
80636 Munich, Germany

Text copyright © Charles Dowding 2026
Woodcut illustrations © Jonathan Gibbs 2026
Copyright © 2026 Dorling Kindersley Limited
A Penguin Random House Company
10 9 8 7 6 5 4 3 2 1
001–358797–Apr/2026

All rights reserved.
No part of this publication may be reproduced, stored in or introduced into a retrieval system, or transmitted, in any form, or by any means (electronic, mechanical, photocopying, recording, or otherwise), without the prior written permission of the copyright owner.

No part of this publication may be used or reproduced in any manner for the purpose of training artificial intelligence technologies or systems. In accordance with Article 4(3) of the DSM Directive 2019/790, DK expressly reserves this work from the text and data mining exception.

A CIP catalogue record for this book
is available from the British Library.
ISBN: 978-0-2418-0710-1

Printed and bound in Slovakia

www.dk.com

This book was made with Forest Stewardship Council™ certified paper – one small step in DK's commitment to a sustainable future. Learn more at www.dk.com/uk/information/sustainability

ABOUT THE AUTHOR

Charles Dowding is a trailblazer in the field of no dig gardening and uses these methods to run his thriving market garden at Homeacres, in Somerset. He started his first organic, no dig garden in 1982, on 1.5 acres at his family's farm, having developed an interest in the link between soil and nutrition while studying at Cambridge University. This venture expanded and, by 1986, Charles was successfully cropping 7.5 acres, and had begun giving talks and writing about his organic growing methods.

Homeacres is Charles's fourth garden, where he continues to observe and reap the benefits of adding a surface mulch of compost each year to feed life within the soil and boost plant growth. While his simple techniques have always grown healthy vegetables and fewer weeds, Charles has also developed his understanding of the processes involved, and his teaching skills too. He has never been afraid to question conventional gardening practices where there is no evidence that they are beneficial, and this "myth busting" approach has helped him develop methods that improve results while saving gardeners time and effort.

Since launching the Charles Dowding YouTube channel in 2013, he has become aware of the amazing potential of new media to share and explain great ideas, information, and the beauty of his work with a worldwide audience. He creates diverse video content to inspire and inform anyone wishing more knowledge of how to grow great vegetables, no dig, and compost mulches. He also continues to produce numerous printed books, and this is his sixteenth.

Charles welcomes visitors to Homeacres to take part in his no dig courses, where they discover the benefits of leaving soil undisturbed, its organisms nourished with compost on the surface, and using no chemical fertilizer or feeds. In recent years, an increasing part of his teaching and trials centres on the themes of this book, growing more plants in less space through overlapping plantings, and closer spacings.